Manual on Being a

Successful Student

Joseph M. Strayhorn, Jr.

Psychological Skills Press

Wexford, Pennsylvania

Psychological Skills Press

www.psyskills.com

author's email: joestrayhorn@gmail.com

Cover art work is a reproduction from Raphael, "The School of Athens," painted about 1510.

ISBN   978-1-931773-14-0

Contents

Why Do You Want to Be A Successful Student?

1. One basketball player loses the ball to an opposing player almost every time he gets his hands on it. He can't ever hit a shot. Dribbling is still a mystery to him.

A second player has perfected shots from every position. He has learned to run at top speed and dribble without even having to think about it. He's learned to get into position automatically each time anyone shoots and to time his jumps so as to grab rebound after rebound.

Which of these two players enjoys the game of basketball more? We can make a confident guess that it's the second. It's fun to do things that you're good at.

The same goes for skills of reading, writing, math, and science. If you get very good at these skills, you will enjoy school much, much more.

What's the purpose of this first section?

A. to persuade you to get better at basketball,
or
B. to give an example of the principle that activities are much more fun when you're more skilled at them?

2. Basketball players who are not skilled and who don't enjoy the game can drop out and not play it any more. People who hate playing piano can decide never to touch a piano again. People who don't enjoy camping out can make up their minds to sleep in a bed indoors for the rest of their lives. With all these hobbies, usually nothing at all bad happens if you totally stop them. It's not crucial to learn to enjoy them.

With reading, writing, math, and other academic skills, however, it's a different story. By law, children and adolescents have to go to school of some sort. There's no way of dropping out of reading, writing, and math.

Why Do You Want to Be a Successful Student?

The main point of this section is that

A. piano playing is not a crucial skill for anyone to learn,
or
B. children can't drop out of the need to learn reading, writing, and math?

3. Why have people made laws compelling people to work for years on reading, writing, math, and science? It isn't because they're mean and like to see people suffer. It's because these skills are very important for living a productive, happy, and fulfilling life after school. At least one of these skills, if not all of them, is necessary for a large fraction of the jobs that are available, particularly those that offer decent pay. Reading and writing are major ways in which people communicate with each other in all their activities, in work and outside of work. Math is necessary for work in science, engineering, or business, as well as for managing personal finances.

A summary of this section is that

A. reading, writing, and math are very important skills for living, both at work and outside it;
or
B. if you want to keep track of your own money, you need math?

4. There's another reason to get highly skilled in the things that schools teach: they can be a source of great pleasure, throughout all of life. This sort of pleasure has been called "the life of the mind." When people read about big questions and major discoveries and important events, and discuss their ideas about these with each other, both in spoken words and in writing, they are participating in the life of the mind. When people try to think up new ideas that will help people or allow us to understand something better, they are involved in the life of the mind. When they try to solve any puzzle, from unscrambling a word to the problem of pollution, and take pleasure when they get a good idea, they are living the life of the mind.

The author uses the term "life of the mind" to refer to

A. taking pleasure from learning and thinking,
or
B. scoring high on tests?

5. The life of the mind is a great pleasure to indulge yourself in. It's not dangerous and is very low in side effects: it doesn't get you fat, cause injuries, damage your liver, make you deaf, or increase your risk of cancer! It is almost always available, because you can never run out of new ideas to learn about and think about. If you get enough pleasure from it, you are less likely to get depressed.

The author seems to be comparing pleasure from the life of the mind with some more dangerous pleasures. Which dangerous pleasures do you think it's more likely that he had in mind?

A. Eating junk food, boxing, driving fast, drinking wine, listening to loud music, and getting suntanned on the beach,

or
B. playing chess, singing with family members, going for walks, and studying nature?

6. If people read widely, look for the most interesting ideas, enjoy talking about those ideas, and find other people who also enjoy talking about those ideas, they are able to have conversations that are a source of pleasure throughout their lives. They never run out of ways to have fun with their friends, or their husbands or wives, because they love to chat with each other. They can connect with each other, rather than sitting with each other staring blankly into space or staring at the television.

The author in this section seems to suggest that learning about ideas and learning to discuss them well

A. helps people to get higher pay,
or
B. helps people to have better relationships?

7. Another advantage of the life of the mind is that when people take pleasure from asking and answering the question, "How can humanity be made better off," they often come up with useful answers! Whether it's the invention of a cure for polio or a recipe for a more nutritious pizza, playing the "life of the mind" game often results not just in pleasure for yourself, but in benefits to others.

The point of this section is that

A. the life of the mind is good simply because it feels good,
or
B. the life of the mind often makes other people better off?

8. Let's return to the more practical reasons for getting very skilled at academics. Many students don't understand why some jobs pay a lot more than others. Why do people who wash dishes or sweep floors or pick grapes get paid less than people who run companies, do surgery, or teach chemistry? It's not that the lower paid work is less noble or good, or less necessary for people. It's that many more people are able to do the first type of jobs than the second. When there are more people to pick from, you don't have to pay them as much. When there are fewer people to pick from, you have to pay them more to attract them.

The conclusion of this is that if you want to get paid a lot, find something that people need very much, that requires such expertise that few people ever learn how to do it well. Most of these jobs start with good skills at reading, writing, or math.

The main purpose of this section was to explain

A. why jobs that require you to be an expert at something that takes a long time to learn pay better than jobs that most people can learn to do very quickly,
or
B. exactly what you need to learn to be a surgeon, and why this takes longer than learning to pick grapes?

9. Do you think it would be more fun to be the president of a company than to be the one emptying the trash cans for the company? Would it be more fun to be a lawyer arguing a case in court than to be the one who washes the lawyer's coffee cup? Would it be more fun to design an airplane, or to vacuum the floor of the airplane after the passengers have gotten off? The first job mentioned in each of these sentences seems like more fun to most people, and it also pays more. This is one of the main things that is unfair in our society: the people with the most fun jobs, who get to think about interesting things and lead other people, also get paid the most for doing them. The people who do the most unpleasant work, like cleaning toilets or working in hot, dirty conditions, get paid the least. This may not be fair, but it is not likely to change within the next century or so!

The people in today's society who get the fun and highly paid jobs are mainly the people with the best educations.

The author's attitude toward the fact that highly paid jobs are also more fun is that

A. this is exactly the way it should be, and the way it will always be, or
B. this is something unlikely to change soon, so it's good to prepare yourself for the interesting and better paid jobs?

10. There's another problem with having one of the least skilled jobs in society. The people who are competing for them are likely to find themselves unemployed. Having no job and not much money saved is a scary position to be in. How will you get food? How do you pay rent on a place to live? How do you pay the gas bill to keep warm in the winter? What happens if someone in your family gets sick and needs expensive health care? The fear of poverty is a very good reason to work hard in school and to get expert at skills that people can't do without.

Why Do You Want to Be a Successful Student?

The reason for working hard in school that the author speaks of in this section is

A. the fear of unemployment and poverty,
or
B. the ability to enjoy understanding complex ideas?

11. You don't have to be unemployed to live in poverty. Let's imagine that someone gets minimum wage in the U.S., which is at the time of this writing, $7.25 per hour. If the person works 40 hours a week, he or she makes around $1200 per month.

But that $1200 won't go far. At least half of it will be needed to rent a decent apartment in many places. This leaves $600. If you have to drive to work, car payments and gas can easily take $300. A phone bill can take up $100. A visit to a dentist will usually cost at least $100. And we haven't even allocated any yet for food or clothing, or for buying anything for yourself. What if a health care need costs you a thousand dollars more? What if you need a $500 repair to your

car? And what if you are trying to support a family as well as yourself?

For this reason, many people with low paying jobs work two jobs and still live in poverty.

The main point the author makes here is that

A. working full-time in a minimum wage job in the U.S. is a life of poverty,
or
B. apartment costs vary greatly depending on where you live?

12. Many children who grow up in relatively well-off families assume that they will be able to keep the life style to which they have become accustomed, no matter what. They don't realize that their money is dependent upon someone's being willing to pay a family member for his or her expertise at something.

Many children who grow up in poverty don't realize that there is a way out of poverty.

Many children from both groups fail to realize that the way to stay out of poverty is to become an expert in some set of skills that people are willing to pay money for. They don't realize that reading, writing, math, and science are the foundations of almost all those skills.

The main point of this section is that

A. poverty subjects people to conditions where people are cruel to one another,
or
B. many children don't realize the connection between academic success and escaping poverty?

13. Many children look at some famous people who get paid very high salaries, and they want to be like those people. Some of these people are athletes, singers, or other entertainers. Children are correct in thinking, "You don't need to know algebra to be a champion football player. You don't need to know chemistry to be a rock guitarist."

But only a handful of people make large amounts of money in sports or entertainment. A fairly small fraction of people can even

earn a living in these fields. Millions of people find that they have worked on sports or entertainment skills for years without being able to earn one penny from their efforts.

With which of these statements would the author probably agree?

A. If you can dream of being a star in a sport or entertainment field, you can live your dream!
or
B. The vast majority of people who hope to earn a living in sports or entertainment are disappointed.

14. There are many, many students who think, "Some people are into academics, but I'm into sports. I'll just get by in schoolwork, but where I really want to shine is on the playing field." There are two things they don't think about. First is the fact that while they're waiting for sports practice, they have about six hours of "getting by" in school to endure, and perhaps a couple of hours of homework to do afterwards. That's a full-time job. It's no fun to have a full-time

occupation in which you're just getting by. If you have to do it, you want to enjoy it, and if you want to enjoy it, you have to do it really well. Getting by is no fun.

The point the author makes about being a sports specialist in this section is that

A. not very many college scholarships are given for sports, or
B. you have a full time job as a student, even if you also do sports, and if you're going to enjoy your full time job, you've got to get good at it?

15. Here's another reason why it's important to get good at reading, in particular. For almost every job or activity that requires you to be an expert, there is a book or set of books that tell you exactly how to be such an expert. Do you want to be a heart surgeon? There are books that tell you exactly how to do each part of this job. Do you want to do research on how the human brain works? There are books that tell you all of what people know so

far about this, and books that tell you how to find out more. But unless you can read really well, and unless you work for a long time at understanding the words used in these books, they will mean nothing to you.

A summary of this section is that

A. whatever you want to be an expert in, there is usually a book telling you how to be an expert, if you can only understand it, or
B. some things you have to see in person rather than read about, if you are going to learn them best?

16. Of course, the ability to read well helps you with all sorts of things other than learning to do jobs. If you can read well, have read about many things, and are interested in many things, there is never a reason to be bored. You can always find something else to read about that is interesting, fun, or useful. There is a huge amount of such information in libraries, bookstores, and on the Internet, and all you have to do is read it. The people whom I hear

complaining of being bored are seldom avid readers.

A summary of this section is that

A. sometimes you have to do lots of tedious practice in reading before it gets to be fun,
or
B. if you can read well enough, you will be much less likely to be bored?

17. If you can write well, you impress people; they tend to think that you are smart enough to do other things well also. On the other hand, if your writing is filled with mistakes and is not clear, you impress people in the other direction.
   But there's another really good reason to learn to write well: writing helps you organize your thinking. Writing helps you remember your own thoughts, and then to put them in a logical order and to make a step-by-step presentation of ideas. When you think without writing, you are limited to what you can hold in memory, but when you think while writing, you can actually think much better thoughts!

The two major points of this section are that good writing

A. impresses people favorably, and helps you think better,
or
B. is used even more than before because of email?

18. I've already mentioned that many careers, such as those in science, engineering, or business, require much skill in math. Another reason to become good in math is that it helps you to become smarter in thinking about all sorts of things that go on in everyday life, and everyday decisions you have to make.

The author's main point in this section is that

A. you need lots of math if you want to be an engineer,
or
B. math helps you think about lots of things in everyday life in a much smarter way?

19. Here's an example of how math helps you think about life more effectively. Suppose that someone is fearful that bad people will break into his house and kill or kidnap him. Someone says, "How many years have you lived at your house so far?"

The answer is, "Nine years."

The other person then asks, "How many times have you been broken into so far?"

The answer is, "Zero."

"And has anything changed over that time about the safety of your neighborhood or your house?"

"No."

The other person then asks, "And on any given night, such as tonight, what do you think is the chance, or probability, that someone will break in, where 0% means it's impossible, and 100% means it's sure to happen?"

The answer is, "About 40%."

If you feel there's a 40% chance that you will get killed or kidnapped tonight, there's lots of reason to feel scared! But if the person were better at mathematics, he would be able to calculate that even if break-ins occurred at a rate of one every nine years for every single house, the probability of one occurring at his house on any given night would be not 40%, but about 3 hundredths of one percent!

This section illustrates the fact that

A. knowing math can help you feel less unnecessary fear,
or
B. knowing math can help you decide when you can spend money and when you should save it?

20. Here's another example of how math helps people to think more effectively. One person thinks: "My Aunt Zelda smoked every day from the time she was 15 years old, and she lived to be 92. She never got lung cancer or any other illness from smoking. That proves that all this talk about smoking causing bad illnesses is just plain wrong. It's part of a big conspiracy."

A second person who knows math better, replies, "The way it works is not that every single person who smokes gets a bad illness. Rather, the probability of getting a bad illness goes up the more you smoke. But there are other variables that also influence that probability. That's why your example doesn't disprove the fact that smoking causes bad illnesses."

If the first person doesn't know enough math, the second person's explanation just doesn't make any sense. The first person may go on thinking a very wrong idea.

This section illustrates the fact that

A. math can help you understand things about the world that everyone should know, such as why the moon doesn't fall into the earth,
or
B. math can help you in thinking in a smarter way about how to take care of your own health?

21. In order to be a successful student, you have to cultivate more skills than reading, writing, and math. These skills are just as important for life as the basic

academic skills are. By making yourself a successful student, you usually make yourself good at these other crucial skills.

One of these skills is organization. Being organized involves keeping track of what assignment is due on what day, keeping track of where you put books and papers, remembering to turn in assignments, and dividing up the work well on long-term projects. It involves planning ahead so as to leave enough time for work. These are skills that are extremely important for most jobs.

The skill, other than reading, writing, and math, that this section mentions is

A. self-discipline,
or
B. organization?

22. Another skill that contributes to being a successful student has been called work capacity, persistence, attention span, mental endurance, and mental stamina. It's the ability to keep working for a long time without rapidly

starting to feel bored, tired, or restless and needing a break. Work capacity contributes to your being successful at any goal you set. It's a skill you can practice and cultivate while becoming a successful student.

The skill mentioned in this section is

A. keeping on working long enough,
or
B. choosing the right things to work on?

23. Self-discipline is the ability to pass up something more pleasant and fun in the present, to achieve a goal in the future. Work capacity is a special type of self-discipline. It takes self-discipline to keep working when you feel like saying, "I've had enough!"

But there are other types of self-discipline that are important for academic work. There's the moment where you decide to start studying, rather than doing something else more amusing (such as watching TV or playing a video game). There's the moment

where you decide to go to bed so that you'll be fresh for a test the next morning, instead of staying up to do something more amusing. There's the moment where you pull the focus of your attention back to your schoolwork, rather than letting it drift into a more amusing daydream.

If you strengthen your self-discipline "muscles" by your schoolwork, this skill will help you to attain any other goal you set for the rest of your life.

A summary of this section is that

A. it's a real shame that schoolwork isn't as amusing at videogames,
or
B. schoolwork gives an opportunity to practice self-discipline skills that will help you throughout your life?

24. Many of the reasons for becoming a highly skilled student involve benefits that will occur far into the future. There's one benefit that is a very present one. In school, you are constantly

asked to perform. Tests, written assignments, answering questions in class, and doing homework assignments are all chances to perform for at least one other person, as well as for yourself. You are being challenged: "Let's see how well you can do this." And you respond, "Here's how well I can do this." Except for those unlucky people who have been able to convince themselves that they don't care how they perform, almost all people have much more fun putting on a great performance than putting on a bad performance.

The main point of this section is that

A. schoolwork involves challenges, and you will have much more fun if you are able to meet these challenges with a feeling of triumph rather than failure,
or
B. if you want to motivate yourself to be a successful student, you should think more about what your future will be like, years from now?

25. Most people would not think of acting in a play without learning their lines well, or performing a solo music concert without practicing their songs until they can perform them really well. It's just too embarrassing to put on a bad performance, and it feels so good to put on a really good performance. The difference in pleasure makes it worthwhile to work really hard to prepare.

It is a different experience to hear an auditorium of people clapping and cheering for you than it is to see an A or 100% written at the top of a piece of paper. But for the best students, the feelings these experiences produce are similar. If you can cultivate the ability to feel really good every time you put on a successful performance, your experience of school will be filled with pleasurable moments.

The author recommends

A. getting into the mindset where you feel really good about every successful performance you put on in school,

or
B. trying to feel very embarrassed about every bad grade, just as if you had made huge mistakes in front of a large audience?

26. Here's another reason why some kids want to be successful students, but it's a tricky one: to get the admiration and approval of your friends.

In the ideal school, all students would support the achievements of all others. Every student could count on a good academic performance getting the same positive reaction that a good athletic performance or a good performance in a play would get.

However, there are many kids who don't get good grades, who want to hang out with kids who also don't get good grades. These kids actually discourage each other from good performances.

There are also lots of kids who do get good grades, who are so competitive that they are jealous of anyone who does better.

So if you want to have friends who will give you genuine congratulations and approval and positive reinforcement when you

succeed, you have to look for them. Some people who look hard still don't find them.

The author's attitude is that

A. if you make good grades, your peers will certainly approve of you,
or
B. some peers may approve of your good grades, whereas others may disapprove?

27. If you have one friend, or one relative, whom you can really trust, you might consider making a secret pact. In the secret pact, you agree that you will not consider yourselves in competition with each other on grades, but that your goal is that the two of you will both do as well as possible. You also agree that when either of you does a good academic performance, the other will try to join in the celebration and congratulations and feel good too. You discuss outright the fact that everyone can benefit from a good audience for their performances, and you try

very hard to supply this motivation for each other.

The author advises

A. looking for a relationship where you can get approval for your academic successes, but not talking about that directly,
or
B. talking directly with someone about giving each other approval for your successes?

28. In this chapter we have discussed many reasons why it is both wiser and more fun to be a successful student than not to be. There are many other reasons that people can come up with. How often do these reasons go through your mind? There are many, many students who if asked to produce reasons why being a successful student is a good idea, would respond with a blank stare or the words "I don't know." Or maybe, if asked why they do their schoolwork, they would say, "Because I have to," or "Because I'd get in trouble if I didn't." These students have a major disadvantage. If you don't have in

mind why you want to do something, it's much harder and less pleasant to motivate yourself to do it.

Which proverb summarizes most closely what the author said in this section?

A. Don't bite off more than you can chew,
or
B. Keep your eyes on the prize?

29. There's another proverb that has to do with the main idea of this chapter: "If you know the 'why,' you're more likely to discover 'how.'" In other words, if you know very thoroughly *why* you want very strongly to succeed at school, you're much more likely to find out *how* to accomplish this goal.

I recommend writing down a list of reasons for wishing to achieve this goal, keeping this list handy, and reading over it very often. When another good reason pops into your head, you add it to the list. This way you make sure you don't forget any of the thoughts that motivate you to do your best.

I've called such a list the "internal sales pitch." You're like a salesperson, trying to convince someone to buy something. Only the person is yourself, and what you're convincing the person to "buy" is high academic skill. The price that is charged is lots of work, planning, and thought.

What's the main idea of this section?

A. It's very useful to keep a written list of reasons for wanting to succeed at schoolwork, and to review this list often,
or
B. it's important not to get involved with a group of friends who put pressure on you not to do well in school?

The Effort-Payoff Connection

30. Many students believe that it would be very nice to get straight A's, to write well, to perform well on achievement tests, and so forth. But what many of them lack is the conviction that there is something they can do, today, that will get them closer to these goals. They feel that things are going to turn out however they turn out, pretty much whatever they do.

Other students have a goal in mind, and they see almost every bit of work they do as getting them closer to that goal. They believe that each little bit of effort gets them a little closer to the payoff they are striving for. They have what is called the "effort-payoff connection."

In this section, the author contrasts two groups of students. What is the difference between the two?

A. One group respects teachers, and the other does not,
or

B. one group feels a connection between the work they're doing and the goal they want to achieve, and the other group does not?

31. Let's imagine two students who have an English assignment on subject-verb agreement. The first student thinks, "I want to be an ace on subject-verb agreement, because I don't want to miss one question on the SAT or ACT that has to do with it, and I don't want one mistake of that sort in any writings I submit anywhere. This assignment gives me a chance to practice. If I miss even one, that points out something I may be shaky on, and may need to learn about. If I get every one right, I've still gotten good practice at deciding the right answer quickly."

The second student thinks, "What do I have to do in this assignment? I'm supposed to pick the right word to go in the sentence. OK, let me get this out of the way. I wish I didn't have so many of these to do.... OK, now

I'm done, I can go play videogames."

The first student is connecting the effort she has to put out on the assignment with a payoff she dearly wishes to get. This student is making the effort-payoff connection. The second student makes the effort-payoff connection only a little bit: this student sees her effort as achieving the payoff of getting the assignment out of the way.

Both students were working for a payoff; what were the payoffs, respectively?

A. for the first, increased skill, and for the second, getting a meaningless task off her back,
or
B. for the first, a top grade on a test, and for the second, the chance to help others in the class?

32. A first student turns in assignments and does tests when he has to. He has no idea what grade he is going to get on his report card until the card comes out. When he does see his report card, he takes fairly little interest in it.

The second student knows how much every test and assignment count toward the grade. Each time this student turns in an assignment or takes a test, he feels great suspense to find out what grade he got on it. He keeps track of every grade he gets, and he recomputes his average often. When the report card comes out, he knows ahead of time exactly what the grade should be, and if there is a mistake, he asks about it.

With regard to grades as payoffs,

A. the first student probably lacks the effort-payoff connection, and the second probably has it,
or
B. the first student is much more motivated by grades than by internal motivation?

33. Why is the effort-payoff connection good? Human beings (as well as almost all other animals) seem to be built so that we are happier if we believe our efforts are getting us what we want. Put another way, it feels good to be in control of things. If

people, or animals, are put in situations where what they do makes no difference in how things turn out, they tend to be less happy, or even to get depressed.

Imagine a video game where no matter what you do with the controls, the game proceeds along in just the same way. You can do nothing to influence it. You lose the game each time, no matter what you do. Or, let's say that you win the game each time, no matter what you do. How long do you think anyone would play either of those games? Not long, because the games can't provide you with an effort-payoff connection, and thus they are no fun.

The main point the author is making in this section is that

A. it takes many hours of effort to become a top student,
or
B. the more you feel an effort-payoff connection, the more fun your efforts will be?

34. One of the major payoffs that your studying and practice effort get you is a knowledge of your own skill, your own competence, in a certain area. In order to feel the effort-payoff connection, you have to first be aware of what skill you are working on. Lots of times when I've asked kids, "What are you learning about in math?" the answer is, "I don't know," or "Lots of different things – I can't really tell you." If a student can say, "I'm working on dividing fractions," or "I'm working on factoring trinomials," that student has a much better chance of feeling the effort-payoff connection. It's possible for the second student to think, "Two weeks ago I didn't know how to divide fractions, and now I do! I feel good about that!" That type of thought strengthens the effort-payoff connection. The student who thinks, "I guess I've learned how to do some things – I don't know exactly what ..." probably doesn't feel nearly as much of an effort-payoff connection.

The main point of this section is that

A. if you want to feel the effort-payoff connection, you should make yourself aware of what skill you are trying to master at any given moment,

or

B. people whose parents pay them money for good grades may have more of the effort-payoff connection?

35. It's good to have an idea, not only of what skill you are learning right now, but where that skill falls on a checklist of skills you need to know. For example, the student who is learning arithmetic might have in mind the following checklist:

1. Understanding place value and how the number system works.
2. Adding, subtracting, multiplying, and dividing whole numbers.
3. Understanding the meaning of fractions, and how you change fractions and mixed numbers to equivalent forms.
4. Doing the four operations (adding, subtracting, multiplying, and dividing) with fractions.
5. Understanding how decimals work.

6. Doing the four operations with decimals.
7. Understanding percents.
8. Doing several types of standard problems with percent.
9. Knowing about time, money, and measures of length, area, volume, mass, weight, speed, and so forth, and be able to solve problems using these measures.
10. Knowing some formulas about how quantities are related in the real world, such as rate * time = distance, unit price * number of units bought = total price, mass/volume=density, and so forth.
11. Being able to do word problems that involve all the above, that illustrate what all this is good for!

This is a very short checklist of math skills, and there are lots of others that could be added. But if the student has in mind, "I want to make sure I can do each one of these eleven skills really well," then each one that the student learns will feel like moving toward a goal. It's as if the student can see the playing field and can see the goal at the end. It's OK that as soon as that goal is reached, other goals will take their place. That's the way life should be.

In this section the author recommends

A. knowing not only what skill you're working on, but also how that skill fits with others on the to do list,
or
B. constantly adjusting your strategy depending on the results you're getting?

36.   Many students have come to view tests as punishment inflicted upon them by mean people. It's not hard to see why this is the case, for students who often do poorly on tests, and come to dread each test as another occasion where an embarrassingly poor grade will come up.

   But the major payoff you get from your effort on schoolwork is the ability to do something you couldn't do before. You don't know that you have a certain ability until you test it, until you meet a challenge with it. For this reason, tests and measures of your ability are your friends, not your enemies. They are your friends because they allow you to clearly perceive the effort-payoff connection. The more you can see measures of your academic ability as your friends, the more likely you are to enjoy being a successful student.

The main point of this section is that

A. tests are meant to measure some academic ability,
or
B. tests, by measuring the results of your efforts, help you see the effort-payoff connection, and are thus your friends, not your enemies.

37. Let's use an analogy to continue to make the same point. Let's imagine two track runners. Each is training for the mile run. The first doesn't own a stopwatch. This runner just goes out and runs, not knowing whether he is getting faster or not. He shows up on the day of the race and hopes for the best.

The second runner owns a stopwatch and uses it very often. Often he times himself on the mile run. He constantly experiments: do I get the best time by trying to run each quarter at the same speed, or should I run the first one faster when I'm fresh? Do I improve my time more by training with lots of fast short bursts, or by running several miles cross-country, or by just running the mile itself, over and over? He keeps track of his best time each week, and enters the results in a table. He knows how fast he needs to get to win races, and he celebrates as he gets closer and closer to that time.

Will the second runner win? Not necessarily. But the second has a much better chance to feel the effort-payoff connection, to feel that his training efforts are actually accomplishing something. He does it by using his stopwatch. For successful students, tests are your stopwatch.

The main point of this section is that

A. just as the track runner uses the stopwatch to get the effort-payoff connection, the student uses tests of academic performance in the same way,
or
B. when you are training for the mile, you should try different ways of pacing yourself, and see which one lets you run the mile the fastest?

38. To most fully enjoy the effort-payoff connection, you have to do your own measurement of your progress. You can't rely totally on your school and your teacher.

In a tutoring program I have run, we've worked with children who were perhaps two grade levels behind in reading, and very far behind their classmates. They got very bad grades in reading. In several months, they made great progress, so as to be only about one grade level behind. But they were still far behind their classmates, and they still got very bad grades in reading! If it had not been for our testing, neither they, nor their parents, nor we tutors would have realized the great progress, the huge payoff, that their efforts had achieved. They might have been so demoralized that they would not have been able to keep working until that major payoff came, where they finally got good grades in reading.

The main point of this section is

A. even poor readers can gain a grade level in several months, with good tutoring,
or
B. you should do your own measurement of progress, and not depend only upon your school to do it?

39. Some other students find that they lose the effort-payoff connection by being too far ahead of their class. They notice that they can daydream during most of the class, rush through their homework assignments without looking at the explanations in the textbook, and get A's on tests without doing any additional work. They have lost the effort-payoff connection because the work is too easy, just as other students lose it because the work is too hard.

This section makes the point that

A. students can lose the effort-payoff connection even when they are getting good grades, if the work is too easy,
or
B. the effort-payoff connection is necessary if students are to really enjoy academic work?

40. If you are in a class that is too hard or too easy, you may want to talk with your parents about trying to get you into a different one where your effort can pay off. Unfortunately, often such different classes aren't handy, don't exist nearby at all, or involve separation from loyal friends.

The author feels that the effort-payoff connection is easier to get if your class is at just the right level of difficulty for you. He feels that getting into this sort of class, if you're not in it,

A. is something that is easily
done,
or
B. is often difficult or impossible
to do?

41. Even if your class is at exactly
the right level of difficulty, and
especially if it is not, you always
can use your own tests and
measures. You can free yourself
from your dependence on school
as the only way of telling whether
your efforts are paying off.

When you test yourself, you
don't have to feel embarrassed
about a "bad grade." If you do
poorly on one of your own tests,
you make a plan for putting out
effort that will help you do better
later. When you take the same test
later, and you see that you can
now do much better on it than
before, you have reason to
celebrate, and you have a way to
notice the effort-payoff
connection.

The main idea of this section is
that

A. you can liberate yourself from
dependence on school tests by
assigning yourself your own tests,
or
B. when you grade the tests you
assign yourself, you should be
careful not to cheat in your own
favor?

42. Research has shown that
students who are frequently tested
remember course material better
than those who are not. The act of
recalling what you are learning is
a skill that improves with practice.
This is another reason why you
want to test yourself more than
your teacher has time to test you!

This section points out an
additional advantage of testing
your self frequently, which is

A. that you can track your
progress and get more of the
effort-payoff connection,
or
B. that you tend to remember
information better, the more you
test yourself on it?

43. Where do you get test
questions? One source is the

questions right in textbooks. Poor students tend to want to do as few of these questions as possible. As soon as the assigned questions are answered, they never want to look at them again.

Successful students view such questions as tests to practice on until they can answer those questions not only accurately, but also fast. If they can't do this the first time, they keep studying the material and practicing the test questions until they can. When you get better and faster at answering these questions, record and notice and celebrate your progress; that's the effort-payoff connection.

This section advises you to

A. use the problems or questions in your textbook,
or
B. make up your own questions?

44. I have heard of students who complained throughout a whole course that their textbook was bad, or that the questions in it were useless. Here's a solution that many students would never even dream of: buy another textbook! On the Internet, you can find cheap, used textbooks on almost all subjects. Even if you have a good textbook, you can often benefit by getting a different author's point of view on the same subject, or different types of test questions. If you see your job as learning the subject matter, and not just carrying out the commands you are given by your teacher, browsing through other textbooks doesn't seem to be such a far-fetched option.

The main point of this section is that

A. being in school does not limit you to one textbook, or any other one strategy of learning, if you liberate your thinking;
or
B. some textbooks may not contain enough of the right types of questions?

45. Another great source of test questions is in a type of literature known as test-prep books. In most bookstores, you will find a couple of shelves of test-prep books for

the SAT test alone, and another couple for the ACT test. There are test prep books for every high school course for which there exists an SAT subject test or an Advanced Placement exam. There are test prep books at the elementary school level – one well-known series is the "Scoring High" series; another is "Spectrum Test Prep" series. These test prep books give you the sorts of questions that many people have agreed are the criteria for success at a given grade level for a given subject matter.

In the above section, the author suggests getting practice test questions from

A. released tests available on the Internet,
or
B. test prep books?

46. There are several other ways of getting good practice test questions.

Sometimes teachers will make available tests from previous years, or study guides.

You can find released tests given by many states on the Internet: just enter into a search engine, released tests state of ___. The state of Texas presents very good data on the test results, as well as many sample tests.

And finally, as you read your textbook or read over your class notes, you can make up your own questions. Making up your own questions has the additional advantage that this activity gets you thinking like a test-maker, and it forces you to process whatever you are reading, to be able to compose good questions.

This section

A. listed three other ways of getting practice test questions,
or
B. advised you on how to use test questions once you have them?

47. There are several other ways of getting the lists of questions or tasks on which you will want to test yourself repeatedly. One important set is the "basic skills" questions – the foundation level

skills that help you with everything else. For example:

1. How fast can you give the one-digit math facts for addition, subtraction, multiplication, and division, when they are presented in random order?
2. How fast can you read aloud a section of text that is appropriate for your grade level, making very few "misreads?"
3. How fast can you type a section of text appropriate for your grade level, using the correct fingers for the keys?
4. Using a list of words appropriate for your grade level, if someone dictates to you a random set, what percent can you spell correctly?
5. How fast can you hand-write a section from some writing appropriate for your age?
6. What percent of a list of vocabulary words appropriate for your age can you correctly define?

These are the sorts of tasks that you want to become "automatic" on – you don't want them to distract you from the more complex activities that involve

them. You want to be able to do them quickly and accurately without even thinking.

The main point of this section was that

A. even though we have spell-checkers, it's still important to know how to spell,
or
B. there are certain basic tasks that you want to become automatic on, so they won't distract you from the more complex tasks that they are a part of?

48. Once you have a list of questions or tasks that you want to master, you want to go through a cycle that we can call test yourself – teach yourself – test yourself..., or for short, the test-teach cycle. This means that you put out effort to learn the skill or the information, perhaps by reading, perhaps by practicing, and then you test yourself to see how much your effort has paid off. You work and practice some more, and you test yourself again. You keep track of how well you did on each

trial. You display the results to yourself in a table or a graph. When you see the numbers going up or down in the direction you want them to go, and when you feel really good about that, you are getting the effort-payoff connection. You keep going through the test-teach cycle until you can answer the questions correctly and fast.

This section recommends that you

A. keep teaching yourself and testing yourself until you can perform accurately and quickly, or
B. keep working until your assignment is done, and then stop, because you are finished?

49. A well-kept secret is that it's OK, and even a good idea, to test yourself with exactly the same set of questions, several times. If you remember exactly how that question was answered before, that's OK! You can get practice this time, answering it more quickly!
    For example, a student takes the math section of a past ACT test, on several occasions. Each time, the student studies the explanations for the answers for each question he missed. Each time there are fewer and fewer problems that the student is shaky on. Finally the student does all the problems correctly, in well under the time limit for the test. Then, the student does the same thing with another past test. This strategy can produce truly winning results.

The point of this section is that

A. you should always work on new questions, not old ones, because it isn't fair to test yourself with questions you've already seen, or
B. it's wise to practice the exact same test over and over till you have mastered it?

50. Sometimes teaching and testing are really the same thing, and you can get lots of time trials in one sitting. For example, you can take a set of math questions and do several trials with them, recording the number right per

minute. You can make a table or graph that comes from your one session of practice. Often you can see big improvement just from one session.

Other of these tables will best be done over a course of months or even years. For example, you repeatedly do practice tests from SAT or ACT test-prep books, and record your percent correct over time.

The point of this section is that

A. the SAT and the ACT have test questions that are really worth knowing how to answer,
or
B. the process of testing yourself and recording the results can be done in as short a time as one sitting, or as long a time as over years?

51. In this process of repeatedly testing yourself, there is a sort of competition. Who is competing against whom? The contest is between your present self, the one doing the test now, and your former self, the one who did the test before. Each time you break your own record, the present self wins.

Competing against yourself is often a much better way of getting the effort-payoff connection than is competing against other people. You can't control how quick and accurate and creative someone else is. No matter how hard you work, there will be people better than you are in almost every academic contest. No matter how little work you do, there will almost always be people worse than you. But if the table or graph that plots your own results shows steady improvement, you know your efforts are paying off.

The point of this section is that

A. competing against your own former self is a great way to measure the payoff of your efforts, as compared to competing against others,
or
B. there are many academic contests that you can find on the Internet, and winning one of these can give you a great feeling of accomplishment?

52. Many students would laugh or roll their eyes at the idea of doing any extra academic work over and above what they are compelled to do for assignments. Many students view school assignments as oppression that is inflicted upon them. Many see those assignments as so painful that they would never willingly give themselves more of such pain.

But one of the main points of this book is that such students need to move beyond the strategy of "minimize the pain." When you have set your own goals, and when you are celebrating each step toward them, you actually enjoy the progress. You want to think in the same patterns as students do who enjoy achieving their academic goals.

To the students who would roll their eyes at the idea of adding more academic work to what they are assigned, this section replies that

A. there is someone else who is competing for the job you will ultimately want, who is willing to do the work you aren't,

or
B. if you set your goals and celebrate the progress toward them, you should be able to take pleasure in the work you do?

53. Having been a teacher myself, I can testify: teachers are human, and we often make mistakes. We can assign work that is not only unpleasant, but also a waste of time.

In my years as a student, the vast majority of papers I was assigned to write compelled me to deal with topics that I considered (and still consider) trivial, useless, and wastes of mental energy. If my writing teachers had simply assigned me to "Think of something useful to say, and write it," my experience would have been much more pleasant and useful.

Nonetheless, I was able to take some pleasure in writing these assigned papers, because I looked at them as practice sessions for the "real thing" – the topics that I would assign myself, the writings I would do not because I had to, but because I had something I wanted to say to someone.

Because I wanted to self-assign topics like "Why People Do What They Do," I could feel some effort-payoff connection from writing about the use of symbolism in a certain novel.

So the self-assigned work, far from inflicting more pain upon myself, was what allowed me to take pleasure in the assigned work!

In this section, the author

A. is still replying to those students who would roll their eyes at the idea of doing academic work other than what they are assigned,
or
B. has moved on to a totally different subject, which is how writing teachers should give more freedom to their students to choose their own topics?

54. Here's one other reply to the students who would roll their eyes at the idea of self-assigning academic work in addition to what school assigns. This is an idea that is important enough to deserve its own chapter. The idea is that if a

certain type of work is very unpleasant for you, you probably have not learned to do it FAST enough.

It would probably be very unpleasant to move a big pile of dirt one teaspoon at a time, for months. It would be much more pleasant to start up a bulldozer and get the job done in two minutes. If you have the basic skills to move quickly on academic assignments, you will enjoy them much more.

The future chapter that is on the idea in this section would probably be called something like

A. Standardized Tests Are Your Friends,
or
B. The Need For Speed?

The Guided Missile Strategy

55. The Chinese philosopher Lao Tsu said, "Weapons are the tools of violence; all decent people detest them." Nonetheless, the image of the guided missile provides the best analogy I can come up with for the strategy I want to talk about in this chapter. Therefore, let's imagine a peaceful use of guided missiles. Let's imagine that a huge asteroid is hurtling through space straight toward a large city on earth. If missiles can hit the asteroid and blow it up before it enters the earth's atmosphere, millions of lives will be saved.

The author in this section is trying to

A. prepare us to use the guided missile as an image that will be compared with something else, or
B. make the point that asteroids can hit earth, and it's good to be prepared for them?

56. There two types of missiles. For the first one, we just aim where we think the asteroid will go, and launch the missile. Once the missile is launched, there's no further control. We cross our fingers and hope that we calculated exactly right.

The second missile is equipped with some sort of mechanism that views the asteroid. If the asteroid is traveling just a tiny bit faster than we thought it was, the missile senses where the asteroid is, and corrects its course. The missile is programmed to continuously sense where the asteroid is, and to recalculate which direction to go in order to collide with it. It explodes only when it senses that it has reached its target.

The second missile has a much better chance of hitting its target, don't you think?

The author believes that the missile most likely to hit its target is the one

A. that goes without correction from where it was originally launched,

or

B. that continually monitors whether it's on the right course and corrects its path so as to keep headed toward its target?

57. Here's an idea for a funny scene in a movie (if someone hasn't already used it): someone makes a soccer ball or a golf ball that is self-propelling and self-correcting, that can be programmed to head toward the goal or toward the hole, no matter what direction you initially propel it. Can you imagine a scene in which the inventor of this golf ball slams the ball in a horrible shot headed toward the woods, but in mid-air, the ball corrects itself, curving to one side and soaring upward, landing on the green, and then steers itself for a hole-in-one?

The purpose of this section is

A. to persuade students to take up golf,

or

B. to give one more image of what something going on a self-correcting course would look and act like?

58. There are some students who are like an unguided missile. They have a certain amount of work per day they are willing to do. They have a certain way of studying each subject, that is the only way that has occurred to them. They have a certain strategy for written assignments, and a certain strategy for taking tests. They have a certain habit of what they do with their mind while in class. They keep using these same strategies, no matter how successful or unsuccessful the strategies are. If they are not doing well in school and not enjoying school, then they figure that's the school's and the teachers' faults.

The author would probably argue that the students who are like the "unguided missile"

A. are never successful,

or

36

B. are successful if the first strategy they pick happens to be a good one, but not otherwise?

59. Other students are like the self-correcting missile. They set goals for how well they want to do in school, and how much fun they want to have doing it. They know that there are lots of different options for how to do their schoolwork. They start a school year taking their best guess as to what strategies to use. But as soon as the first tests and compositions start coming back, they immediately rethink their strategies. Here are some of the things they might think: "I memorized many more details than I needed to for this test. The next time, I can skip memorizing so much, focus on the big ideas, and enjoy the subject more." "I knew how to do the math problems, but I was too slow at them. Before the next test, I need to practice going faster." "This test asked a bunch of things that were in the textbook, but weren't mentioned in class. I need to study the textbook more."

The students who use the self-correcting strategy

A. always study textbooks rather than just relying on class notes, or
B. adjust their strategies depending on the results they get?

60. The most fundamental self-correction strategy is this: if you are making bad grades, work more. If things aren't going well, sink more time and effort into: first, planning how to make things go better, and second, trying out the plans you have made.

The same advice applies to everything else in life. How can you improve the strategies you are using for your career, your marriage, your health, your relationships with each of your friends, the clutter in your living or working space, and so forth? If things are not going well, put time into figuring out your options for making things better, and time into executing the plans you've made. When the missile is off course, invest effort into getting it back on course. And if it's right on course, celebrate that and feel good about it!

Which of the following is the *opposite* of what the author is recommending in this section?

A. Read what others have found out about how to improve things,
or
B. just keep doing whatever you're doing and don't change it, and if things don't work out well, just stay the course?

61. Before you can use the guided missile strategy, you have to decide what your target is. Many students are content to get "Mostly A's and B's, and a few C's," but still would like to go to a highly selective university such as a member of the Ivy League. Reality is quite a bit different from their hopes.

If you would like to get into any of the 40 or 50 most selective colleges or universities in the U.S., you have to get pretty close to straight A's. What's more, the courses you have to get A's in have to be almost all "honors" or "Advanced Placement" courses –

that is, the hardest ones that a high school offers. On the ACT or SAT test, you probably have to get a score better than those of about 90% of all other students to have a shot at these selective schools.

A summary of this section is that

A. if you want to get into one of the top rated colleges in the U.S., your grades and test scores have to be not just good, but outstanding,
or
B. the ACT and SAT are the two major standardized college admissions tests given to high school students?

62. However, it is possible to get an excellent college education from any of hundreds of U.S. colleges that are not nearly so hard to get into as the top names that the top students seem to want. But in order to get that "excellent education," the students have to use excellent work habits in their college courses. They don't pick up these work habits by being lazy and specializing in video games throughout high school.

It is also possible to live a very useful and happy life without even going to college, but by going directly into job training or a job. On the average, the college graduates make lots more money, and get more interesting jobs. But there are notable exceptions to this rule.

This section

A. continues to argue that you must get straight A's in high school and close to perfect scores on college admission tests,
or
B. makes the point that getting less than top grades in high school does not rule out a successful college career nor a happy and useful life?

63. In my opinion, one of the best reasons to set your sights on an A grade for a course, and a very high score on standardized tests, is that school is much more fun that way. It's not fun to be asked even one test question that you don't have any idea how to answer. It is very much fun to go through a test at good speed, getting question after

question right. It's very much fun to write an essay fast, telling ideas that you feel enthusiastic about.

In this section, the author advises setting your sights on high grades because

A. school is more fun that way,
or
B. there is great competition for jobs, and the people who have gone to the best colleges will get them?

64. If you are reading this book, you will probably want to set your sights on very high grades on standardized tests like the SAT and the ACT. You'll probably also want to aim high for similar standardized tests such as the Terra Nova, the Iowa Test of Basic Skills, the Stanford Achievement Test, and so forth. Part of the reason is that the skills tested through these are very much worth knowing! All of these tests measure your ability to

1. read sections of text, on various subject areas, and answer

questions that test whether you understood what you read;

2. recognize correct and incorrect writing, for example grammar and capitalization and punctuation and sentence structure;

3. do math problems.

The SAT and ACT also measure

4. your ability to write a quick essay on an assigned topic.

These skills have not been selected for these tests without good reason! These are the skills that will continue to help you throughout all the education you receive for the rest of your life. These skills will also help you in almost any job you take.

The author's belief is that

A. standardized tests are overemphasized, unfair, and should be eliminated,
or
B. standardized tests measure skills that are very much worth knowing, and the time spent perfecting these skills is very well spent?

65. There's another reason why standardized tests are your friends. You may have a teacher who "grades hard" or "grades easy," or who gives grades that depend mainly upon something other than learning the material (such as remembering to turn assignments in, or having a good attendance record). You may be in a school where it is very hard or very easy to get an "A" grade. But in half an hour to an hour at home, you can take a test in a certain subject from a test prep book or a released test on the Internet, and get a good picture of how you compare with other people your age all over the country.

The main point of this section is that

A. released standardized tests and test prep books allow you to get a picture of how "on target" you are, that is more accurate than grades alone,
or
B. practicing and studying for standardized tests allows you to do much better on them?

66. Once you have chosen your target, you take aim at it. Some successful students purposely start out the school year working *too* hard. When they find themselves getting great grades on tests and papers, but spending a little too much of their lives doing so, they adjust their course toward giving themselves more free time, by finding out which sorts of work they can skip. They adjust their level of work downward, but if they overshoot and get a bad grade on one quiz, they immediately correct their strategies.

The purpose of this section is to point out that

A. when you adjust your strategy, you don't always decide to work more -- sometimes you decide to work less;
or
B. the faster you are at reading, writing, and several types of basic math problems, the more fun schoolwork will be for you?

67. If you are going to decide how to adjust your strategies, first you have to know what your current strategies are! If someone asks a student, "What strategies are you using now for doing well in your math course," and the student replies, "I have no idea what that question means," or "I don't know," then that student is at a major disadvantage.

Here's what you talk about when you review for yourself what your strategies are.

1. How much time you put in.
2. Where and when you put in that time.
3. Exactly what you do when you are putting in that time – what you do with your hands and eyes and mind.

In this section the author defines "strategies" for schoolwork as

A. how much time you spend, when and where you spend that time, and what you do during the time,
or
B. which teachers you have, where you go to school, and when you graduate?

41

68. So, for example, suppose someone says, "My strategy for math is to do my homework problems for 20 minutes a day, during the commercial breaks of the television show I watch from 8 till 9 every night; I work the problems without even looking at the explanations or sample problems in the book, and without checking my answers. I put my homework paper in my backpack at some random time later, if I happen to think about it. During math class I do my English assignment which is due the next period." Then at least that student knows what his strategies are. If those strategies are getting fantastic results, then it's hard to argue with success; otherwise, I'll bet you can think of ways the strategies might be changed!

The author probably admires the way this student

A. does homework during TV commercials,
or
B. knows what strategies are being used?

69. If you are not doing well enough in schoolwork, what possible strategies can you change, to get back on the right course? Here are three general types of strategies:
1. Work for a longer time.
2. Accomplish more per minute worked.
3. Get more credit for what you do accomplish.

We'll think about lots of more specific options, very soon. But they all fall into one of these categories.

The three categories mentioned in this section are

A. three reasons why it is important to adjust your course when you are not doing well enough,
or
B. three general ways to get back on course when you are not doing well enough?

70. One of the major reasons for failing in any sort of goal is simply not logging in enough time working on it. If your grades or

practice test scores are too low, you probably need to increase the amount of time you spend working on your schoolwork.

Researchers have studied what leads to people's becoming high achievers in various fields of work. One of the major findings is that "time on task" makes a huge difference. Those who log in more hours working to get better at something, achieve more at it.

How many days per year do Olympic swimmers go without working out? Except for the days when they are very sick, the answer is approximately zero.

The concert pianist Paderewski was asked about his practice time. He said, "If I go one day without practicing, I notice it. If I go two days without practicing, the critics notice. If I go three days, the audience notices." Studies of successful concert pianists confirm that in addition to natural talent, they share a commitment to practice, every day, for hours, not just a few minutes.

The main point made by this section is that

A. high achievers tend to spend lots of time practicing their skills, or
B. you need a certain degree of natural talent to be among the highest achievers in lots of skills?

71. I have heard some kids say, "I shouldn't have to work on schoolwork at home. I put in enough hours working during the school day. Other workers get to relax after work when they come home, and I should too. Six hours or so, five days a week, should be enough hours to learn all you need to know."

I do think that six hours of highly efficient, concentrated effort per day should be sufficient for most younger students to learn what they need to know. But for most students, many of the hours of school are not efficient, concentrated learning time. For most of the best students, the hours they spend at home are the most efficient learning hours they spend.

There's another problem with the "no work at home" reasoning: the people who believe in it are being compared with other people who don't feel this way. In the competition for grades, admission to college, and high-level jobs, the people who feel that no work should be done after school tend to be the losers and those who feel differently tend to be the winners.

Finally: most of the very high-achieving people in rewarding careers do not log in just eight hours a day, five days a week, and relax the rest of the time. The "time on task" rule applies in the world of work as well as the world of school.

In this section, the author gives three arguments for the idea that

A. if the work is concentrated and efficient, you can accomplish school in much less time than most people usually spend,
or
B. doing work at home after school and on weekends is an essential part of being a successful student?

72. There's one problem with increasing the time you spend working: you have to spend less time doing something else. What

are you going to do less, so that you will have more time to study?

To answer this question, think about where your time does go – what activities do you do? If you rank order them, which ones fall at the bottom of the list with respect to how pleasant, useful, or otherwise worthwhile they are? If there are television shows you watch but don't enjoy much, or video games you feel are a waste of time, these are excellent candidates for activities to stop doing in order to make room for more studying.

A summary of this section is that

A. if you want to be a successful student, immediately cease watching TV and playing videogames,
or
B. if you need to spend more time studying, think which activities give you the lowest payoff, and replace some of the time spent on them with study time?

73. How can you get more learning out of each minute you put in on schoolwork? Let's talk

about how to read a textbook. If you are lucky enough to be highly interested in what you are reading, simply sitting and reading a chapter or section of the text from start to finish may be highly efficient for you. But if you find that your mind is wandering, and if you find that you get the end of a page of reading the text without remembering much of what you have read, you need a different strategy.

The general idea for all the "different strategies" that we'll talk about is to alternate between trying to take information in, and testing yourself to see whether you succeeded.

One of the ideas of this section is that

A. you should be able to simply read your textbooks, enjoy them, and remember them, without using special techniques,
or
B. special techniques can very much help you absorb what's in your textbooks, and these techniques have to do with testing

yourself to see what you remember?

74. Here's one of several such strategies. It's called the reflections exercise. You read a paragraph of text, and then, without looking at the text, you write down the main ideas from what you read. (Paraphrasing what someone else has said is called doing a "reflection.") If you aren't sure you got the reflection right, you reread the paragraph to check your work. In reading the paragraph, you are trying to take information in, and in doing the reflection, you are testing yourself to see whether you succeeded.

The reflections exercise is, according to this section,

A. one of several ways to alternate between learning and testing your learning,
or
B. the only way to alternate between learning and testing your learning?

75. Here's a variation of the reflections exercise that you can

use during a "work party" with a "study buddy." You both read the next paragraph of the text, either silently or aloud. Then one of you does a reflection, aloud. Then you both read the next section. Then it's the other's turn to do a reflection, aloud. If either of you wants to add (or subtract) anything to or from the other's reflection, just do so, or if you want to reinforce the other's reflection as masterful, just do that.

The purpose of this section was to

A. define what is meant by the reflections exercise,
or
B. describe a way that two people can do the reflections exercise together?

76. Here's another way to alternate between learning and testing your learning. You read, and as you read, you write down questions over what you have read.

   Of course, answering the test questions is a way of testing what you have learned. But even before you do that, you test yourself just by seeing if you can come up with a good question. If you read a section of text and think, "What question can I ask about that? I don't remember anything at all worth asking about," then either your textbook included a somewhat unusual section, or your mind was wandering and you missed at least one important point that you could have asked a question about.

One of the major points in this section is that

A. you test your understanding of a section of text just by seeing if you can make up a question about it,
or
B. you don't really test yourself until you reach the end of the chapter and see if you can answer your own questions?

77. Some students have fun with making up questions, by turning the activity into a game of "Let's see how well I can anticipate the real test questions." The student tries to guess what the teacher will

ask on a test, and then compares this guess to the real test. Armed with this experience, the student can make even better guesses the next time around. By the end of the course, the guesses are sometimes right on target.

The purpose of this section was to

A. explain exactly how making up questions forces you to process the information very actively,
or
B. describe a variation on question-making, which could be called "Guess the Test Questions?"

78. Here's another technique that often gives you more comprehension per minute spent studying. It's asking yourself, how does what I'm reading fit in with the rest of what I'm learning? How do the parts fit together to make a whole? Someone who makes great use of this technique spends time contemplating the table of contents of a textbook, and notices and thinks about the chapter headings and subheadings. Other people ignore all these

signals, and treat a textbook as if it were one long string of text without the organizing aids.

The point of this section was

A. keep asking and answering questions, any questions, while you are studying,
or
B. keep trying to notice how what you are studying fits in with what you have learned before and what you will learn in the future about this topic?

79. Someone using the "How does it fit together" technique with the book you are now reading may think something like this: "The first chapter discussed why being a successful student is desirable, and what the payoffs are. The second chapter talked about the link between effort and the payoff. This chapter is telling about how to stay on track toward the payoff, and now we're going into different things to do to get back on track if you get off. We've talked about the spending more time, and now we're into ways of making time pay off

more. So far, we've mentioned the reflections exercise, making up questions, and now the 'How does it fit together' technique – all of these are ways to be more efficient."

Someone using the technique described in this section

A. concentrates on each part of a textbook, trying to empty the mind of the other parts so they won't be distracting,
or
B. often thinks about how the various parts of a textbook relate to each other?

80. Here's another way to get more learning out of each minute you spend working: eliminate distractions. Don't even think about watching TV while you do your work. Don't have messaging popping up on your computer or your cell phone. Don't try to work and carry on a conversation at the same time. I recommend not having music playing in the background. If there is unavoidable noise in the background, you might consider buying and using noise-canceling headphones.

Some people think that they are good at multitasking, or that they can only work when they are dividing their attention between something and something else. This is almost always not the case. It may take some time for some people to get used to working distraction-free, but after a few days, for almost all of them the work is much more efficient.

The author feels that

A. you have to experiment to see whether you work best with the TV on or off,
or
B. you should just assume that you'll work best with the fewest distractions, and you'll almost always be right?

81. Here's a technique that's very useful for math, physics, chemistry, and any other subject where problem-solving is a major part of the game. This technique seems so obvious that it seems silly to even have to say it, but

sometimes it seems like a well-kept secret.

The technique is NOT to go straight to the assigned homework problems and start working on them. Instead, first read the explanations carefully. Study any worked-out sample problems, and then solve the sample problems and compare your answer to the book's solution. Repeat this process until you fully understand the explanations and sample problems, and then go to the assigned problems.

The advice this section gives on learning problem-solving is to

A. spend careful time on your text's explanations and solved problems before going to assigned problems,

or

B. avoid using a yellow highlighter, because you ruin your book for anyone else?

82. Here's a way to get more accomplished per minute that you work on writing assignments: learn to be very fast both in handwriting and typing. You don't want the mechanical act of writing to slow you down. You want to be able to think a sentence and magically see it take shape in written words, without having to think about the individual letters at all! This is very possible, if you work on your skills of handwriting and typing until they become automatic.

If you could choose just one of these to get very fast in, typing would win out over handwriting, because the world has moved to computer communication, and will move farther in that direction. But at the time I'm writing, most tests in most schools, as well as the SAT, ACT, and AP exams all require students to handwrite their essay responses.

The advice in this section is to

A. become very fast at thinking up ideas,

or

B. become very fast at converting words in your mind to written words?

83. Another technique for getting more efficient in written

assignments is called GIOW. To use this technique, you don't try to write the finished product all at once. First you generate ideas, writing down your thoughts as fast as you can. Then you figure out which you want to include in your essay, moving the others out of the way for now. Third, you arrange the ideas in order. And fourth, you work on the wording, spelling, capitalization, punctuation, and so forth. GIOW stands for generating, including, ordering, and wording.

GIOW stands for

A. different stages of the process of writing something,
or
B. different reasons why it's good to become a skilled writer?

84. The idea of GIOW is that many people write slowly and painfully because they are trying to do everything at once. They get a good idea and write it down, but feel bad because it is worded awkwardly. But the brain can work most efficiently if it pays attention to one thing at a time.

So, for example, you forgive yourself for any awkward wording until you are ready to do the last stage of revision. Until that time, you focus on what you want to say, and in what order you want to say it.

The theory behind GIOW is that

A. you only have so much working space in your brain, and it's good to apply it to one task at a time,
or
B. you will tend to do things more often if someone else gives you some approval?

85. When you have done lots of writing for a very long time, your reward is sometimes that you can depart from GIOW. You begin to get more automatic with your spelling, sentence construction, grammar, etc., and you tend to organize your ideas more automatically – so that your writing tends to come out closer to the finished product, the first time around. The sooner you can get to this stage of writing

development, the more you will really enjoy writing.

The author feels that you

A. should follow his GIOW writing plan for the rest of your life,
or
B. can make the skills of writing more and more automatic over a long time, so that it becomes more possible to do the four writing tasks at the same time?

86. What else can you do if you find yourself getting off track? You can get help, from a family member, a friend, a teacher, or a professional tutor. You can repeatedly rate your own concentration, and see how high you can get it and how long you can keep it high. If you have ADHD, you can take medicine for it. If your dose of medicine is too high or too low, you can work with your doctor to try to get it right. If you think your textbook is bad, you can buy a different one. If you think the class is too hard or too easy, you can try to move into an easier or harder one. If the work is too hard, you can do extra work on easier skills, the easiest ones that you are a little shaky on. If you think the work is too easy, you can get it out of the way at high speed and then do some more learning that's more challenging for you. If other people are distracting you, you can try to shut yourself up in a room by yourself. If you are getting too lonely while working, you can try to find a study buddy who can work silently with you and keep you company.

A title for this section might be

A. Distractions are Not Good,
or
B. Other Miscellaneous Suggestions on How To Work More Efficiently?

87. Sometimes the problem is not that you are not learning efficiently. Sometimes the problem is that you are not getting credit for the work you do.

Suppose that someone is learning the information in the textbook very well. But suppose it turns out that the tests in the course do not cover the textbook at all, but ask about information the teacher talks about in class. If this student could possibly get a bad grade, not because she was not learning, but because she was learning the wrong stuff!

This section gives an example of someone who is

A. not learning,

or

B. learning, but not learning the right stuff to get a high grade?

88. Many students have no idea how their teacher comes up with their grade. The formula for the grade is called the "grading rubric." Here's a simple one: the two in class exams each count 25%, and the final exam counts 50%; a score of 90 to 100 is an A; 80 through 89 is a B, and so forth.

What does it mean when scores count a certain percent of your grade? It means that to get the final number, you multiply each score by the percent that the score is weighted, and add up all those products to get the final score. So for example, if with the rubric

above, the student got 80 on each of the in class exams and 100 on the final exam, the final score would be .25*80 + .25*80 + .50 * 100, or 90. So the student would just barely get an A, according to the grading rubric.

The purpose of this section is to

A. explain how grading rubrics are used to assign grades,

or

B. persuade you that teachers should just report percent scores and not use letter grades?

89. Can you imagine a successful football player who does not know how many points the team gets for a touchdown, a field goal, an extra point after a touchdown, and a safety? Or a successful basketball player who doesn't know or care which shots get one, two, or three points? Similarly, the most successful students pay lots of attention to how many points they get for what – they are aware of how their grades are computed.

The major idea of this section is that

A. if you play football, you should make sure you know how many points you get for what,
or
B. as a student, you should know how your teacher computes your grade?

90. Most successful students also pay lots of attention to exactly what they have to do to get the grades they want. When they have a test, they make sure they know exactly what information the test will cover, and what sorts of questions will be asked. When they have a written assignment, they want to know exactly how the teacher will judge it. How much emphasis does the teacher put on neatness, correct grammar and spelling, good sentence structure, good use of words, and good ideas? They don't want to spend lots of time figuring out the most eloquent way of expressing something, for example, if the teacher's rubric involves a list of major ideas and simply checking

off whether the student mentioned that idea or not.

This section suggests that students ask themselves which of the following questions?

A. How will the information in this assignment help me to help my fellow human beings?
or
B. If I were grading this assignment, exactly how would I come up with the grade?

91. There's one other major task for students who want to get credit for what they know: turn in your homework! There are several different steps in this task. Each of these steps must be completed successfully in order to get credit for the homework. This is such an important topic that I've devoted the entire next chapter to it.

The author suggests that

A. turning in homework should be very simple and easy for everybody,
or

B. getting credit for homework involves doing each of several steps successfully?

92. If you remember the different strategies in this chapter, you should be able to list many different ways in which you can get back on track as soon as you notice yourself getting off track. But in order to use these strategies best, you have to keep asking yourself, am I on track? Am I getting behind? Is my learning very effective? Am I on schedule to have fully mastered the skills of this course, by the time it ends? Answering these questions well requires being honest with yourself. It can take some real courage to be able to say to yourself, "I've fallen behind in this." or "I don't really understand this well enough." or "I can do this, but I'm too slow at it." or "I've been goofing off too much." or "I need to get some help on this."

Being able to admit things like this to yourself is hard. It's a test of how tough and brave you are. Many students can't do this at all. They just go along and avoid asking themselves the question of whether they're on the right track, either because the question has never occurred to them, or because they fear admitting to themselves what the answer will be. If you can have the courage to ask this question, and the self-discipline to use the strategies mentioned in this chapter whenever you notice yourself off track, you are much more likely to be an academic winner!

A major purpose of this section was to

A. sell the reader on having the courage to honestly answer the question, "Am I on the right track?"
or
B. make the point that if a course is just too hard, you learn lots more being successful in an easier course than by being totally confused in a harder one?

Avoidance Versus Mastery

93. How often do you ever think the words, "I'm at an avoidance versus mastery choice point?" Probably for most people, the answer is "Never." But these choice points are extremely important for becoming a successful student and for enjoying your academic life. This chapter will tell what these choice points are.

This section

A. defines the meaning of avoidance versus mastery choice points,
or
B. says that avoidance versus mastery choice points are very important?

94. Imagine that Ed finds math very unpleasant, because it is very hard for him to remember the math facts such as 8+9 or 7x6. When there is an assignment, it is tedious for him to count up or use a calculator or otherwise make up

for his skill deficiency with these facts. The tedium and frustration of doing math problems are very unpleasant.

When something is unpleasant for us, the natural response is *avoidance*. Avoidance means that we get away from, and stay away from, the unpleasant situation. For Ed, this might mean rushing through the math assignments, or not doing them at all, and spending no time on math that he isn't absolutely compelled to spend.

This section

A. explained what mastery is,
or
B. gave an example of avoidance?

95. Here's another example of avoidance. Tina has never done much writing. She's very self-conscious about her writing, because some people have been very critical of her early efforts. So she finds writing very painful.

As a result, she avoids writing unless she is compelled to do it, and even then she puts it off as much as possible. Putting it off makes it even more unpleasant.

This section

A. gave another example of avoidance,
or
B. talked about exactly how often vicious cycles caused by avoidance are present when students fail?

96. Now let's imagine that each of these students decides to give up the avoidance strategy and go for mastery. Ed decides to work on math facts for a few minutes every day until they come quickly and easily to him. At first this work is quite unpleasant. But as he keeps at it day after day, he gets used to the work. Gradually, as he gets faster and better at the math facts, the work crosses the line into actual pleasantness. The rest of his math work also becomes more pleasant also. In the mastery strategy, he worked on the skill that was in short supply, and with greater skill came greater pleasure.

The thing that enabled Ed to cross over from avoidance to mastery was

A. hypnotic suggestions that math facts are fun,
or
B. enough work on math facts that he got really skilled at them?

97. Suppose that Tina gets a writing tutor, and works every day on writing. She starts with easy tasks and works her way up to harder ones. At first, the very thought of working on writing is very unpleasant for her. But as she works on it day after day, the unpleasantness subsides. Over time, she actually learns to enjoy writing.

This example of mastery has which of the following in common with the previous example?

A. that the person worked under the close supervision of a tutor,
or

B. that the person got lots of exposure to the situation he or she had the urge to avoid?

98. Suppose someone thinks, "If I spent time working on this, I would probably get used to it, and more skilled at it, and it would get more pleasant. But in the short run, it would be very unpleasant." This person is at an avoidance versus mastery choice point. The person is at that crucial place where he or she has to choose whether to use the avoidance strategy or the mastery strategy.

   Is the mastery strategy always better? Not necessarily. You can't master everything. Once I went to a folk dancing lesson, where the steps were just too complicated and difficult for me to enjoy the activity. I've avoided that particular type of dancing for the rest of my life, and I'm glad I have. I could have used the mastery strategy, but I just didn't enjoy that type of dancing enough to put the time into it.

This section makes the point that

A. sometimes you'll want to choose avoidance over mastery,
or
B. there is one right answer whenever you're at an avoidance versus mastery choice point?

99. For dancing and camping and sports and chess-playing and all sorts of other hobbies, avoidance is often a perfectly fine strategy if you don't like the activity. But for math, writing, reading, spelling, getting organized on turning in work, test-taking, and other crucial academic skills, the mastery choice usually makes things turn out much better than avoidance. You often just can't avoid the activity, even if you'd like to.

This section emphasizes the point that

A. there are certain academic skills where the avoidance strategy just doesn't work,
or
B. many, many people use the avoidance strategy with important skills, even though avoidance doesn't work well?

100. Using the mastery strategy is somewhat like going through a tunnel.

Suppose that you are walking on a long journey, and you come to a tunnel. The tunnel is the only way to the other side of a huge mountain with cliffs so steep they can't be climbed. The tunnel is dark and scary and the path through it is less pleasant than staying outside. But, let's imagine that, because you've been through this tunnel before, you know that you only have to endure a limited time of dark and scary travel, and then you'll be delivered to the other side of the huge mountain.

On the other hand, someone who has never been through this tunnel, and especially someone who has never been through any tunnel, might hesitate to enter. How does that person know the tunnel actually comes out on the other side, rather than just going deeper and deeper into the earth? That person would be more likely to wander around outside and to put off entering the scary tunnel, and never to make it to the other side.

The strategy that is being compared to going through a tunnel is

A. the avoidance strategy,
or
B. the mastery strategy?

101. In the same way, someone who has never had the experience of working at difficult and unpleasant tasks until they become easier and more pleasant, may not know that pleasantness and mastery are even possible. The person may think, "I have always hated doing math facts, and therefore I always will." Or the person may think, "No matter how much I work on writing, I will always hate it and be bad at it."

For this reason, it's very important that on even one occasion, you can have the experience of working at something difficult and unpleasant until it gets easier and more pleasant. This experience will give you the faith that the mastery strategy is possible, and that it can be rewarding.

This section's main point is that

A. the avoidance strategy gets to be a stronger habit the longer you use it,
or
B. even one experience of working at something hard and unpleasant until it becomes easy and pleasant can help you have faith that the mastery strategy can work?

102. Many of us have had successful experiences with the mastery strategy that we've forgotten or that we ignore. If we can bring them back to mind, particularly when we are at an important avoidance-versus-mastery choice point, this can help us.

For example, Ted is having trouble with keeping his work organized and turning it in. He thinks about the strategy of paying lots more attention to how he organizes, and how well he organizes. He recalls a time when he was first learning to read, where it was unpleasant to try to read aloud. He remembers that the more he worked on reading, the more pleasant it became, until he could finally very much enjoy reading fun books. Recalling this experience helps him have the confidence that the "tunnel" really can come out on the other side of the mountain.

The major point of this section is that

A. if you remember your past successes with the mastery strategy, you'll have more faith that it can work,
or
B. learning about other people's successes with the mastery strategy can be another way of knowing that it can work?

103. Larry is at an avoidance versus mastery choice point. He very much dislikes reading aloud in front of people, or giving speeches in front of people. He purposely recalls a time when he found it difficult and unpleasant to try to ride a bicycle. He recalls that as he kept working, he broke through into the promised land where riding the bicycle became

easy and pleasant. This memory helps him to have faith that if he practices reading aloud to others enough, it will get easier and more pleasant.

This section is another illustration of the fact that

A. recalling successes with the mastery strategy helps us have faith that it can work,
or
B. the more we avoid a task, the less of a chance we have to develop skills in it?

104. Of course, not all tunnels come out on the other side of mountains. Similarly, you can't always be sure that keeping on working at something will get you to the promised land where the work is easier and pleasant. If you were to give the average second grader a college physics book and urge the student to keep working until the work was easy and pleasant, the likely result would be only discouragement. To make the mastery strategy most likely to work, the skills should be within the student's reach – not too hard,

and not too easy. When this is the case, the student finds before too very long that at least some tasks are starting to get easier and more pleasant.

The main point of this section is that

A. for the mastery strategy to work, the student has to at least give it a chance by working some,
or
B. for the mastery strategy to work, the tasks the student works at should be not too hard or easy, but at a "just right" level?

105. Most students never think about whether they are at an avoidance versus mastery choice point. Most never consider whether the mastery strategy is likely to work. Most never consciously think about what order to work on things so as to give the mastery strategy the best chance of working. Most never purposely recall the past successes of the mastery strategy, so they can muster the faith necessary to do some unpleasant work. But you can think about all these

things, partly because you now know some words that you can use to ask yourself these important questions.

The main point of this section is that

A. it takes great courage and fortitude to make the mastery choice,
or
B. the words you've learned in this chapter can help you ask yourself useful questions that most students never ask themselves?

The Art of Turning In Your Work

106. Some people get bad grades, not because they are not learning, but because they can't get their act together to turn in their assignments. There's a chain of tasks that are necessary if you want to actually turn in your work. Here it is:

1. You have to hear or read the assignment.
2. If it isn't already written down (e.g. on the internet or in a syllabus), you have to write it down, someplace where you can find what you've written (such as an assignment book).
3. You have to get your assignment book home with you, if you're going to do the work at home.
4. You also have to take home with you any books or papers or other materials you need to do the work with.
5. You have to find what you did with your assignment book and books, once you get ready to work. (This is easier if you put them in the same place each day.)
6. You have to do the work.
7. Assuming you do the work on paper, you have to put it in whatever you take things back to school in (such as your backpack), preferably in some sort of organized folder.
8. You have to take the backpack with you when you leave for school.
9. You have to show up at the class where the work will be turned in, with your backback (or your folder) with you.
10. You have to remember to take the work out of whatever it's in, and hand it over to your teacher.

A slip in any one of them can result in a missed assignment.

Why do you think the author lists these steps necessary for turning in assignments?

A. To convince you how difficult it is to get assignments turned in, or
B. so that if you have trouble getting assignments turned in, you

can analyze which step causes the problem?

107. Your goal is to establish a routine for each one of these steps: that is, you want to do each of these in as close to the same way, each day, that you can. That way you get into a habit that leads you to do these automatically, without thinking about them. So for example you use the same assignment book and the same backpack each day. You put the backpack at the same place each day when you get home. You put the work into a folder and into the backpack immediately after doing it. You leave the backpack in the same place each time you finish your work. You get the backpack from that place at the same time each morning, before you leave. And so forth.

The reason for trying to establish a routine is

A. so that you will develop a habit so strong that you don't have trouble remembering any of these, or

B. so that you will be more and more aware of what you are doing in each of these steps, as time goes by?

108. If you have trouble getting assignments turned in, it's a good idea to figure out: which of the above steps are being done well, and which of them are not. Then you do lots of fantasy rehearsals of any step that isn't being done well.

A fantasy rehearsal, if you're not familiar with it from other books in this series, is a practice that you carry out in your imagination. You imagine yourself carrying out the action just as you want to do it in real life.

If you speak in words what you are imagining, telling the situation and your thoughts, emotions, and behaviors in response to it, and your celebration of your positive response, you are carrying out the STEBC of fantasy rehearsal. (STEBC stands for situation, thoughts, emotions, behaviors, and celebration.)

The advice in this section is that

A. if you have difficulty with a certain step in the process of getting work turned in, do lots of fantasy rehearsals of performing the step well,
or
B. if you have difficulty with a certain step in the process of getting work turned in, try to remember when your bad habit got started?

109. Let's suppose someone figures out that the weakest link for her in the homework-turning-in chain is putting the completed homework in the backpack. Here's how she might do a fantasy rehearsal:

I'm in my room, and I've just finished writing an essay for English. I print it out, and I check it over, and it looks good. I feel good about my work.

But now, wait – I'm not finished yet. I need to put it in my backpack, so I won't forget to take it to school! I'm glad I remembered to do this, and decided not to put it off. I get my backpack, and get my English folder out of it. I put my essay in the folder, and put the folder back in the backpack. Now, I'm really finished with the assignment! Hooray, I did it!

The purpose of this section is to

A. give an example of how to do a fantasy rehearsal,
or
B. convince you that fantasy rehearsals change real-life behavior?

110. So far we've talked about breaking the task of turning in work into its parts, and rehearsing in fantasy any part that sometimes is skipped. There's just one more point to make about suspense.

The people who forget to turn in their work often seem to have something in common: a lack of a feeling of suspense about the grades on their work. If you can build up that feeling of suspense, you'll be more likely to turn things in.

Imagine two people. The first is thinking, "I've gotten 100%'s on the last five homework assignments I've turned in. Can I keep my streak going? I hope so!"

And I think I've got a good chance! I think I did all this homework correctly, and I checked it well. I can't wait to find out whether I aced this assignment!"

The second has no idea what the last five homework grades have been. When you ask this person, "What grade do you expect to get on this homework assignment," the person shrugs and says, "How should I know?"

Which person is more likely to remember to turn in his or her homework?

A. the first,
or
B. the second?

The Need for Speed

111. Think of the people you know who most enjoy running. Do they run fast, or are they very slow?

How about the people who seem to enjoy talking with people the most. Do they speak quickly, and can they think of things to say quickly, or do they take a long time between each word?

How about people who greatly enjoy playing a musical instrument? Can they add a new song to their repertoire relatively quickly, or is adding a new song a very slow, painstaking process?

You can probably think of more examples of the following principle: there's a connection between the pleasure you get from an activity and how fast you are able to do it.

Another example of the principle that is given in this section is that

A. people tend to enjoy community service more when they get to see someone actually becoming happier,

or

B. people who do lots of reading for pleasure tend to be able to read faster than those who don't enjoy reading?

112. I believe that there is something built into our brains that makes it pleasurable to accomplish a lot quickly, and makes it painful to do long labor without seeing much result. Probably our prehistoric ancestors who took pleasure from cultivating crops faster by using plows and oxen survived at higher rates than those who were content to dig the ground with sticks. Probably those who took pleasure from transporting things by carts with wheels survived and thrived much more than those who were content to carry as much as they could load on their shoulders.

The author's theory is that

A. people who enjoyed getting things done faster probably were more successful in surviving throughout human history, and thus probably we all have something built into our brains that makes us enjoy getting work done quickly,

or

B. when you do a task slowly, you get to think about it more, and it's more pleasant?

113. There are certain things that it's important to take your time doing. When you have to make a very important decision, or complete an assignment that represents a bunch of important decisions, it's good to be able to devote to the task the time it needs. If you're doing scientific research, for example, you need to plan carefully how you will get your data, analyze it, and write it up. If you are writing a story, you will produce a better one if you devote time to figuring out who your characters are and what they're going to do. You can't accomplish everything at breakneck speed.

The point of this section is that

A. you should be able to accomplish every academic task very quickly,

or

B. there are certain tasks where it's much more important to make good decisions than to make fast ones?

114. Nonetheless, there are certain academic tasks that you want to be able to do very quickly. One reason to get fast on certain skills is that they are the skills that you will be using on standardized tests. Standardized tests almost always have a time limit. One can go along answering every question correctly, but still do very poorly on the test, if one is so slow that many questions are left unfinished.

The reason for cultivating speed that was mentioned in this section is that

A. speed is a sign that you are able to do a task without having to devote so much of your "working memory" to the task,

or

B. standardized tests are almost always tests of speed as well as of accuracy?

115. Here's another reason for getting very fast at certain academic tasks. The faster you can do these things, the faster you will complete assignments. You will have more time to do other things. Part of those other things may be relaxing, goofing off, socializing, and having fun. But some of the "other things" you will have time to do may include drilling yourself so as to get fast at some other important task, using a textbook or test prep book other than the one you are assigned, or going back to earlier sections of your courses and reviewing.

Imagine two students. The first one gets assignments done so slowly that he would never even consider doing something that is not assigned. The second gets assignments done so quickly that there is at least half an hour per day to review things already learned, practice doing things faster, prepare for tests in the distant future, and to master important skills that have not been

assigned lately. The difference in the success of the two students is likely to be enormous.

In this section, the author gives a reason to learn to do academic tasks quickly: it is

A. that you will have to learn the material very well in order to do tasks quickly,
or
B. when you can do homework quickly, you will have time for self-assigned important work, as well as more time for fun?

116. Now let's think about another reason for teaching yourself to be fast in academic tasks. This has to do with "working memory." Working memory is how many new bits of information you can hold in memory at once. If someone reads out a list of random numbers or letters and asks you to repeat them, the person is testing your working memory. All of us have limitations on our working memory. We can remember almost unlimited amounts of information if we have time to

review it and rehearse it, and to do what is called "consolidating" it into "long term memory." But for unrelated bits of new information, somewhere between three and nine things is the limit for almost everyone.

If an actor memorizes lots of lines that she will speak in a play, the information is held in

A. long term memory,
or
B. working memory?

117. Now please imagine two students who are taking a math test. One of them has memorized the multiplication facts so well that she can recall them instantly. When she sees 7 x 8, the number 56 effortlessly pops into her head.

The other has ways of figuring out the answer. When this student sees 7 x 8, she thinks, "8, 16, 24, 32, 40, 48, 56," and counts as she does so, stopping when she has made skip-counted 7 times.

The second student has to hold several things in working memory. Did I decide to skip count by 7's, or 8's? Am I going to stop after 7, or after 8? If any of the steps in the skip-counting is shaky, then the student has to add, and thinks something like "48 + 8 is the same as 16 plus 40, which gives 56." But this absorbs memory also, and the student is likely to think, "Now I know the next step is 56, but I've forgotten how many times I've skip-counted."

Suppose that multiplying 7 x 8 is only one step in a series of steps that needs to be carried out in order to solve the problem. The first student is not wasting working memory on 7 x 8, and can devote more working memory to holding in mind a plan of how to get the answer to the problem.

The main point the author is trying to illustrate is that

A. when someone doesn't have quick strategies for certain academic tasks, the tasks absorb working memory that could better be used in other ways,
or
B. skip-counting may be OK for learning the multiplication facts,

but eventually you want to memorize them?

118. Trying to do tasks without enough working memory is extremely unpleasant. Probably everyone has had this feeling from time to time: it's as if you're juggling, but there are way too many balls. You figure something out, but by the time you figure it out, you have forgot the other thing that you needed to hold in memory that you were going to do with it once you figured it out! When people get the feeling that their memory resources are hopelessly overloaded by a problem, most tend to avoid it altogether.

The point the author is making here is that

A. trying to do a task without enough working memory to do it is not only difficult, but quite unpleasant,
or
B. you can extend your working memory by writing things down?

119. Here's the crucial connection between working memory and speed: The ability to perform a task faster and more automatically is usually a sign that the task isn't absorbing as much working memory.

For example, when a beginner uses a computer to write, the mind devotes a certain amount of working memory to thoughts like, "Let's see, where is the letter k? Oh, yeah, the home key for my right middle finger. But I want capitalize it, so I push down the shift key with my left little finger...." and so forth. But the expert typist simply thinks the words, and out they come onto the computer screen, without devoting any thought to which letter is in which position. A great deal of working memory has been saved. Writing is much more pleasant.

The author seems to imply that the solution to the problem of memory overload is to

A. increase your working memory,
or

The main point of this section is

B. make certain skills so automatic that they don't absorb working memory?

120. Typing is one of the *component skills* for writing. A component skill is one of several different skills that go into carrying out a more complex task. Let's give some other examples: Running fast is a component skill for playing basketball; jumping high is another; throwing the ball into the hoop is another. For being a star in a musical play, singing, dancing, and acting are all component skills. Each of these has its own component skills: for example, in singing, correct pitch, good pronunciation of the words, and a good tone are all component skills. And for producing a good singing tone, correct breathing techniques, a good position of the larynx, and opening the back of the throat are all component skills.

The main point of this section is that

A. if you want to sing well, you should work on good pitch, good pronunciation, and a good tone,

or

B. complex skills can be broken down into the component skills that are necessary to carry them out, and the component skills can be similarly broken down?

121. What's the point of thinking about the component skills that combine to make more complex skills? The big idea is that if you are finding the process of learning a skill frustrating, you probably should go back and work on one or more of the component skills until you make them fast and automatic. For example, if you are working on high school math, but you are very shaky on your basic facts such as 7 x 8, you should go back and get fast and automatic on the basic math facts.

The main point of this section is that

A. it's much easier to learn complex skills if you're fast and automatic at each of the component skills,

or

B. it's important to know quickly how to multiply 7 x 8?

122. Let's list some of the tasks that you need to be able to do quickly, and make some estimate of how much speed you should shoot for.

One of the most basic tasks is reading aloud. When you are reading lists of individual words, a speed of about 50 to 70 words per minute is a standard. (The same speed is a standard for reading off the most common sounds of individual letters.) You can go faster reading connected text: I recommend shooting for a speed of about 150 words per minute, when reading aloud from textbooks at your grade level. Some people can get up to 200 or even 250 words per minute. Of course, there are many component skills for reading aloud. One is called "word attack," and it means the ability to look at combinations of letters, whether they are real words or not, and make a good guess as to what sound the letters would make. A second component skill is vocabulary learning – it's difficult to read words fast if you aren't very familiar with what they mean. And a third component

skill comes just from practicing reading aloud, seeing the words and getting them to come out of your mouth. Finally, the skill of adjusting your tone of voice and inflections so as to fit the meaning of what you are reading and the punctuation on the page, is a complex skill.

The complex skill that is the main subject of this section is that of

A. using inflections of voice properly,
or
B. reading aloud?

123. How fast should you be able to read silently? This depends very much upon how difficult the material is that you are reading. But for material that you have absolutely no trouble understanding, a silent reading speed of over 400 words per minute is very helpful.

The author probably thinks that silent reading speed should be

A. considerably faster than the speed of reading aloud,

or

B. at least 400 words per minute, even with very complex text such as explanations in a hard math book?

124. For writing, it's good to be able to both handwrite and type. A component skill for handwriting is simply making letter-sized vertical straight marks, and letter-sized circles. A standard for writing a series of straight marks by hand is 240 per minute, and for making circles is 100 per minute. Then for handwriting, as in writing words, copying text, or writing the alphabet over and over, a standard is 80 legible letters per minute.

For typing, 5 characters (including spaces) are counted as a word. A beginning typist who is skilled enough not to be terribly distracted by the typing task can type accurately at about 20 words or 100 characters per minute. An expert typist can get up to 50 words per minute or over, which is 250 characters per minute.

The author believes that

A. one should not worry about handwriting, because typing (or keyboarding) has totally replaced it,

or

B. it's good to get fast at both handwriting and typing?

125. Many students develop their own pattern of correspondence between fingers and keys when typing. That is, they may use the first two fingers, or the first three, and may sometimes touch a certain key with one finger and sometimes another. This is a big mistake. As soon as possible, you should learn to type each key with the "correct" finger. When you type this way, each time you type, you are strengthening a memory trace for where the keys are. When you type a letter sometimes with one finger and sometimes with another, your memory traces interfere with one another. If you want to get to be a fast and automatic typist, use the "correct" fingers for each key.

The author's main justification for learning to use the "correct" fingers for the keys when typing has to do with

A. strengthening all four fingers, or
B. letting memory traces get strengthened with each practice rather than interfered with?

126. What are the "correct" fingers for the keys when typing? It's possible to tell this very quickly. The home keys for the left hand are a, s, d, and f, which are typed by the little, ring, middle, and index fingers respectively. The fingers stay on the home keys when they are not typing another letter. For the right hand, the home keys are j, k, l, and ; which are typed by index, middle, ring, and little fingers respectively. This covers the home row, except for g and h: you type g with the left index and h with the right index.

Then you look at the diagonals of keys going to the *upper left* and the *lower right* of the home keys. The same finger that types the home key types the keys in those diagonals. For example, the left little finger types not only a, but z and q and 1. The left ring finger types not only s, but also x and w and 2. The ten diagonals to practice are aqaz, swsx, dedc, frfv, gtgb, hyhn, jujm, kik, lol., and ;p;/.

When you want to type a capital letter (or a character written on top of the key, when there are two of them) with one hand, you use the little finger of the other hand to hold down the shift key. You type the space bar with the thumb of the right hand.

And that's the total of what you need to teach your fingers to do!

The author feels that the knowledge of which fingers you should use with the keys on a computer keyboard is

A. something that can be told only in a book of its own, or
B. fully contained in the section above?

127. How do you teach your fingers to use these keys? There are many systems of learning, but here's one of the simplest.

You start by typing asdfg hjkl; over and over, until you can do this very quickly.

Then you type the diagonals: aqaz swsx dedc frfv gtgb hyhn jujm kik, lol. ;p;/ over and over until you can do this very quickly.

Then you type the alphabet: abcdefghijklmnopqrstuvwxyz over and over until you can do this very quickly.

"Very quickly" means about 100 characters per minute or over. Of course, with all three of these exercises you are very careful to use the correct fingers.

Then you practice making capital letters for a while, and then you start copying any text you want, again concentrating on using the correct fingers. It helps to type the same few sentences over and over until you get them very fast, and then practice with another sentence. From here on out, all the typing you do will help you get faster and faster.

The main purpose of this section is to

A. remind you to use the correct fingers when you are practicing,

or

B. outline a plan of teaching yourself to use the correct fingers when you type, using a few basic exercises?

128. How do you measure how many characters per minute you can type? All you need is a word processor, a watch that measures seconds, and a calculator. You start timing, and type whatever you want. You stop timing whenever you want. You see how many seconds have passed. Then you have the computer count the number of characters you have typed. You can select the passage that you have typed, amid a larger file, by either holding down the left mouse button and dragging it over the passage, or holding down the shift key and using the arrows to darken the passage. Then, in Microsoft Word, you use the "tools" menu and select "word count." The resulting box will tell you the number of characters (including spaces). You divide the number of characters by the number of seconds to get the characters per second, and

multiply the answer by 60 to get the characters per minute.

Figuring out how many characters you have typed

A. involves counting each letter or space, and is fairly tedious,
or
B. can be done quickly using the "word count" function on a word processor?

129. You can use the same "word count" function to measure your speed at most of the other tasks we've mentioned so far. You can find a passage on the Internet that you want to use to time your reading or handwriting, for example, then copy and paste it into a word processing file, and then count the words and characters. You start timing, read or copy the passage, and stop timing. You divide the total words or characters by the number of seconds it took you, and multiply by 60 to get words or characters per minute.

The point of this section is that

A. "word count" on a word processor will help you measure reading and handwriting speed as well as typing speed,
or
B. counting a "word" as five characters probably gives more accurate comparisons for speed on different passages?

130. How fast should you be able to do the basic math facts, when they are mixed up together? By basic math facts I mean problems such as 8+9, 16-7, 9 x 6, and 56/7. If you are looking at the facts and saying the answer out loud, I would shoot for about 80 per minute. If you are looking at the facts and writing the answer, I recommend shooting for 60 per minute. I have written a math facts program where you choose the correct answer by picking the correct answer from two choices and typing either 1 or 2 on a computer; for this method of entry about 40 per minute is good enough, because the mental process of coding the answer to a 1 or 2 takes up a little time.

The purpose of this section is to

A. explain the reasons for getting fast on basic math facts,
or
B. give some standards for speed on basic math facts?

131. There's another set of questions that I recommend drilling on repeatedly in math, until you can do them much faster than you did them at the beginning – perhaps several times faster. These are whatever problems your textbook gives you, whatever homework problems you have, whatever typical test problems you will do. Many students consider their math work done when these problems are written down and finished. But if you want to be the best possible math student you can be, your work includes doing at least some of these problems more than once, in time trials. Can you do them with complete accuracy, almost as fast as you can speak or write?

The point of this section is that

A. it's good to view a math problem set as not something just to finish, but to learn to do fast,
or
B. in order to do complex math problems fast, you have to first be fast at the component skills?

132. Here is one more suggestion about something with which to do repeated time trials. Find a practice standardized test for your level, from a test prep book or from a released test on the Internet. Take the practice test. Then score your test, and study the explanations for each question that you missed or guessed on. Take the test again, aiming for 100% accuracy.

Now you are not finished, but you are ready to begin! You can now do repeated time trials with this same test, until you can answer all the questions accurately and very fast. You want your brain to have the experience of moving fast and comfortably through just the type of questions you will face.

If you can do this with several different tests, you not only will boost your test score – you will boost very important academic skills that will help you in everything you do in school!

This section advises

A. doing practice tests from test prep books, or from released tests on the Internet, one after another, or
B. doing the same practice test repeatedly, until you are fast and automatic at it?

133. If you try doing repeated time trials and you find that you don't increase in speed, and the task doesn't get easier and more automatic quickly, you probably need to "go down the hierarchy of difficulty," or work on the component skills that go into whatever you are trying to do. This may mean going back and doing problems that you studied a long time ago, but did not master.

A summary of this section is that

A. if repeated time trials don't get you faster, you probably need to work on easier component skills till you get fast on them,

or
B. it's good to learn the art of working at top speed while at the same time relaxing?

134. Here's another very important strategy when doing repeated time trials. It's called "biting off a smaller chunk." If your speed is not increasing as you do more time trials, maybe you're trying to load too many bits of information into memory at once. Try cutting down the number of items that you're practicing with, until you can see your speed rapidly increase.

  For example, suppose you're doing time trials with math facts. You practice with all 100 of the "0 to 9" addition facts, but your speed isn't increasing. So instead, you pick out 10 facts and do repeated time trials with just these. You find your speed rapidly improves.

The main point of this section is that

A. it takes courage and self-discipline to do repeated time trials,

or
B. if your speed doesn't improve rapidly while doing repeated time trials, try "biting off a smaller chunk," or practicing with fewer items?

135. If you find that your speed rapidly improves when you practice with 10 math facts at a time, you may want to see what happens with 20 at a time. On the other hand, if the speed still doesn't improve rapidly, you might want to drop down to 5 facts at a time. You have the attitude of a scientist, doing experiments upon yourself, searching for just the best sized chunk that will help you learn fastest and most pleasantly.

The main idea of this section is that

A. it's good to experiment to find out just the right number of items to practice with on any given task, or
B. one of the benefits of repeated time trials is that they get you used to being timed, and help you not to find that unpleasant?

136. Some students never, or hardly ever, do repeated rehearsals with the same task. Many students have an aversion to practicing the same task even twice in a row. Some students say, "But I've already done that!" in a tone of voice that implies that once should be enough for any one task. The idea of practicing the same task ten or twenty times in a row would be the last thing they would consider doing.

What if a basketball player had the same attitude? "I've already practiced a foul shot once. I don't want to do it again." Or a musician: "I've already played that song once. I don't feel like doing it again before the performance." Or an actor: "We've already rehearsed that scene one time. Why on earth should we need to practice it again?"

In this section the author is

A. trying to convince you of the value of repeated rehearsals in academics, by making analogies with sports, music, and acting,

or

B. trying to help you be a better basketball player by pointing out that foul shots should be practiced thousands of times?

137. If you can make repeated time trials a routine part of your learning, you increase your chances for success greatly. You do a task and time yourself. You divide how many you did by the number of seconds and multiply by 60 to get the number you did per minute. Or, you may want to simply record the time. Then you do trial two, with exactly the same task. Are you faster already? If so, you greatly celebrate. You record the results of trial two. Now you do exactly the same task in a third trial. You see how low you can get your time, or how high you can get your number of units done per minute. You aim for a certain feeling, when you can do the work not only accurately, but quickly and with much of it done automatically.

In this section the author is trying to

A. make sure you realize which subjects NOT to do repeated time trials in,

or

B. make sure you know exactly what is meant by doing repeated time trials?

138. The ability to tolerate, and even enjoy, repeated rehearsals and repeated time trials is one of the things that separates the "winners" from the "losers" in the academic arena. Few students have the self-discipline to do repeated time trials. Now that you know this secret, I hope that you can use it!

The main point of this section is that

A. you have to be the one to decide how many time trials are enough,

or

B. those who can do repeated time trials are more likely to be "winners" in academics?

139. Here's one of the most important tips in this book. I've made this point before, but it's

worth repeating. Suppose there's a subject, such as math or writing, that you don't enjoy. I'll bet that if you become much faster at it, and all the component skills involved in it, you'll enjoy it much more.

Many students go wrong by getting into a vicious cycle, as follows. They don't enjoy a subject. Therefore, they avoid doing it. Because they avoid it, they don't get to practice the skills enough to get fast and fluent in it. This keeps them not enjoying it.

If you can make a reflex connection that tells you: "I'm not enjoying this – I need to get much faster at it, and its component skills" instead of "I'm not enjoying this – I need to avoid it," – this reflex can make a major difference in your life!

The main idea of this section is

A. if there's a subject you don't like, rather than avoiding it, work to get faster and better at it,
or
B. if there's a subject you don't like, try to find out from another student who likes it, what makes the student like it?

140. There are some subjects that you can successfully avoid. If you sign up for basket weaving or belly dancing or karate and find that you hate studying the subject, then you can drop out of the course with the knowledge that these skills are not important for success. But for the vital skills for success, such as reading, writing, and math, avoiding the subject is usually not a good option, and mastery is by far the better option. For vitally important skills, the choice often comes down to this: do I want to continue to dislike this and try unsuccessfully to avoid it, or work to master it and enjoy it?

The main idea is that

A. people have done lots of research on why work is more pleasant when you are more skilled at it,
or
B. for reading, writing, and math, unlike some other skills, avoidance is not an option, so

you'd better learn to enjoy them
by getting good at them?

Peak Performance on Tests, and Overcoming Test Anxiety

141. Some people study hard for tests, until they feel they know the subject matter thoroughly. But when the test comes, they get nervous, or freeze up, or otherwise fail to achieve peak performance. They walk out of tests feeling disappointed, and later they grimace to find that they have missed test questions that would have been easy for them at any time other than in the performance pressure situation.

This section is referring to people who

A. have simply not put in enough time studying,
or
B. have studied for enough time, but can't perform well enough during the test itself?

142. What do we mean by "test anxiety?" Anxiety is about the same as fear. If, while taking a test, you feel your heart pounding, your hands sweating, your breathing going fast, your muscles tensing, and your hands trembling a little bit, you know that your body is perceiving itself to be in danger and is pumping out adrenaline in order to prepare you to meet the danger by fleeing or fighting – thus you are experiencing the "flight or fight" response. This is a very common response to fear.

The point of this section is that

A. test anxiety means a fear of taking tests, and the adrenaline response to tests is the usual reaction to scary situations,
or
B. you can learn to control the flight or fight response by doing enough relaxation and biofeedback practice?

143. The more adrenaline you are pumping, the more you feel excited. Excitement can sometimes be pleasant, and it can sometimes help you achieve your

best score. It's possible to be too relaxed, not excited enough, when taking a test. But it's also possible to be too excited. The mental state you are in when you are ready to sprint away from a predator is not necessarily the mental state that will most help you come up with answers to math problems! You are seeking a level of excitement that is not too high, not too low, but just right for the particular task you are doing.

This section implies that

A. the more psyched up and excited you are, the worse will be your performance on a test,
or
B. there is a certain level of excitement that will help you do best on a test – not too high, not too low, but just the right level?

144. What do we mean by peak performance? We mean that in the situation where your performance "counts," for example the real test, you do about as well as, or better than, you have done in your best practice performances. We mean that the excitement of

knowing that this is the "real thing" does not hurt your performance, and even helps it.

The main purpose of this section was to

A. define what is meant by peak performance,
or
B. make the point that too much excitement and arousal can reduce the quality of your performance?

145. The guidelines I'll present in this chapter are useful for all sorts of performances in addition to tests. Job interviews, music or drama performances, sports contests, and public speaking are all situations calling for peak performance where others are watching or monitoring your performance.

The main idea of this section is that

A. the guidelines in this chapter should help with all sorts of situations where you want peak performance,
or

B. if you want peak performance, you should teach yourself to control your own level of arousal?

146. When you take tests, peak performance means that you perform on the real test about as well as, or better than, you have performed on practice tests. In order to do this, you have to have done at least one practice test in the first place!

In your practice tests, you want to practice doing as close as possible to *exactly* what you will be doing on the test itself. If you will be writing several essays with an average of seven minutes allocated to each, you want to practice writing essays at that pace. If you will be solving problems with the help of your calculator, and then picking the correct answer from five choices, at the rate of at least one problem per minute, then you want to practice doing exactly that.

The first guideline, offered in this section, is that you should

A. practice with tasks that resemble the "real performance" as closely as is possible,

or

B. remind yourself that your performance on the test is not a life-or-death matter?

147. When you start doing practice tests, you should take as much time as you need to answer the questions accurately. But it's important that you eventually practice answering questions at the speed that you will have to answer them on the real test. Some students practice test questions without creating time pressure for themselves, and then when they take the real test, they find themselves in a situation that feels totally different. When you're in a situation where every second counts, you want to have practiced performing in this circumstance. If there is a certain watch or timer that you will use during the test, I recommend using that same timer during practice tests.

The main idea of this section is the guideline that

A. you will want to focus on each test question without worrying about the previous or upcoming questions,
or
B. in practice tests, you should practice performing with a time limit?

148. When you do practice tests, it's useful to go, if possible, to the very room where the test will take place and do a practice test there. If this is not possible or convenient, you can still do something that is possibly even better: you use your imagination to take the practice test under the same conditions as the actual test. You imagine the room where you will take the test. You visualize your fellow students around you. You visualize the teacher giving instructions and presenting the test questions to you. You start the clock, and imagine that it is timing the real test.

The guideline spoken about during most of this section was

A. imagine yourself in the actual test conditions while you take your practice test,
or
B. wear the same clothes and use the same pen or pencil that you will use during the actual test?

149. In attempting to duplicate the conditions you will experience during the actual test, the most important, of course, is the test questions. You want to practice with questions that are as similar as possible to the questions you will encounter on the test. Where do you get these? Here are some possibilities:
1. Previous years' tests
2. Test prep books
3. The questions you have been assigned for homework
4. The questions or problems presented in your textbook
5. Types of questions used in previous tests in the same course
6. Questions your teacher has given in anything other than homework, such as study guides
7. Questions you yourself make up
8. Questions you find on the Internet (especially upon typing

the phrase "released tests" into your search engine)

This section presented a list of

A. different ways to prepare yourself to achieve the right degree of excitement,
or
B. different sources for practice test questions?

150. What's the point of making your practice test experience resemble as closely as possible the actual test? One reason has to do with skill-building: you want to practice just the skills you will need on the test. But the second reason has to do with reducing anxiety. How do you reduce anxiety? Three of the most important words about reducing anxiety are *prolonged exposure* and *habituation*. Exposure means that you put yourself into, or expose yourself to, the scary situation. That is, if you want to get over being anxious about tests, you put yourself into the test situation. Prolonged exposure means that you stay in the situation for a long time, not just a brief exposure. And habituation is what happens after prolonged exposure: you get used to the scary situation, and you can handle it in a more relaxed way. Habituation means "getting used to it."

So if you want to get over anxiety about tests, you will want prolonged exposure and habituation to just the sort of test conditions that make you anxious.

This section makes the main point that

A. you get over anxiety by prolonged exposure and habituation,
or
B. practicing relaxation can not only reduce anxiety, but also be a pleasant way to spend time?

151. Each time you do a practice test, you vividly imagine yourself taking the real test. You rate whether your level of excitement is

very much too high
somewhat too high
just right

somewhat too low

very much too low.

Over time, excitement and anxiety that are too high should become lower, because with prolonged exposure comes habituation. It helps to notice the anxiety level go down as you practice more.

This section contains advice about

A. what to do during the real test
or
B. what to do during practice tests?

152. How do you know how much excitement is "just right?" You try to remember, or write down, how much excitement you were feeling, and grade your own practice tests. You see how much excitement seems to lead to the highest scores on the practice tests. This is the level that is the "just right" level you want to shoot for on the real test.

The purpose of this section was to

A. remind you that you should try for the "just right" level of excitement,
or
B. help you figure out what the "just right" level of excitement is?

153. Some students find that there's a part of them that resists going to the "just right" level of excitement when the stakes of the test are high. It's as though a part of them is saying, "What are you doing relaxing? Don't you know this is so important? This is an emergency—you need to act and feel like it!"

It's good to recognize that inner voice, if it does exist, and calmly to reply to it. An example of the reply might be, "But I've already figured out that more excitement is not necessarily helpful and can take away from my performance. I want to work close to the 'just right' level of excitement that I've already discovered."

The main advice given in this section is to

A. recognize and reassure any part of yourself that seems to feel that

you *should* feel extremely excited and scared,
or
B. speak calmly to yourself when emergencies happen?

154. As you take your practice tests, (and as you take real tests) regularly take just a fraction of a second to use "self-reinforcement." That is, when you feel sure you have gotten a question right, you don't just go on to the next one. You say to yourself something like, "Yes! I got it!" and you try to feel good about that success.

Why do this? First, when you're feeling proud of yourself and excited about your successes, it's hard to feel a great deal of fear at the same time. The feelings of celebration are not compatible with a high degree of test anxiety. If you can practice associating positive feelings with test-taking, this is one of the most important things you can do to make success more likely.

Second, taking practice tests is something you'll want to do a lot. The more you celebrate your successes, the more you will enjoy your practice tests, and the more you enjoy them, the more often you'll be able to do them.

This section offers two reasons why

A. you should celebrate and feel good about your successes as you take tests,
or
B. you should take a large number of practice tests?

155. As you take tests, here's a thought to flash upon that might help you celebrate and feel good about your successes in answering questions: "How long ago was it that I would have had no idea how to answer this question? And now I can answer it perfectly! That's progress!" You don't want to go into great detail about this, because you don't have time – you want to practice just an instantaneous awareness that the fact that you can answer the question you just answered is a sign that you're growing and improving and getting more skilled.

Another way of expressing the thought that this section advises flashing upon is

A. "I'll be able to use this knowledge to help people!"
or
B. "I've come a long way!"

156. The next guideline is a technique you can use whenever you want to reduce your fear of any situation. Before going into the situation, you ask yourself, "How would I *like* to feel in that situation?" For example, instead of scared, you may want to feel determined, focused, excited, confident, or proud of yourself. Then, you recall or imagine situations in which you've felt just the way you want to feel, and you picture those scenes vividly. You then visualize yourself going into the new situation, feeling the same way you felt before. Finally, you actually go into the new situation, bringing into it the feelings you've decided you want to have.

In the technique this section describes, you

A. relax your muscles to turn down your level of excitement,
or
B. recall or imagine situations when you felt the way you want to feel, so as to bring those feelings into the new situation?

157. Let's go through an example of how to use this technique for a situation other than test-taking. Suppose someone is set to put on a musical performance, and is nervous. The person asks, "How would I like to feel?" The answer is, "I'd like to have fun, feel excited, and enjoy the way the music sounds." Then he searches his memory for times when he's felt this way. He remembers a time recently when he had a jam session with some friends, and he had a great time making music that came out sounding good. He vividly recalls this experience, and how he felt. Then he imagines himself performing, feeling much the same way. Finally he actually performs, bringing those feelings with him.

The purpose of this section was to

A. present a new guideline for overcoming test anxiety,
or
B. to give an example of the technique that was described in the previous section?

158. If you are searching your memory for times when you felt the way you want to feel while taking a test, hopefully you won't have to search very long. Hopefully your practice tests will provide just those memories – especially those practice tests where you have performed and felt the best. If, during those practice tests, you have felt excited but not too excited, proud of yourself for the answers you are getting right, and totally focused on the question you are answering, then it's good to relive those memories just before the actual test. You visualize yourself feeling the same way while taking the actual test. Then you do take the actual test, bringing those feelings with you.

What does this section advise you to do just before the actual test?

A. remind yourself that the test is not a life-or-death matter,
or
B. recall how you felt taking your most successful practice tests, and visualize yourself feeling the same way while taking the real test?

159. Thus just before you are taking your practice tests, you vividly imagine that you are taking the real test. Just before you take the real test, you vividly recall taking a practice test. After you've done this for a while, your images of taking the real test will include images of recalling the practice tests. And your memories of practice tests will include imagining that you are taking the real test. Thus your images of the real test and practice tests will become more and more intertwined with one another. That's a good thing – you want to import into the practice tests the energy and excitement of the real tests, and you want to import into the real tests the relative calm and feeling of safety you have during practice tests.

This section describes

A. something good that might happen after you've used these imagination techniques for a while,

or

B. several reasons why you should focus completely on the question you are answering at that moment?

Don't Waste Energy During the Test On Painful Emotion

160. Suppose you come across a test question on a subject you neglected to study. Many people would think, "Why did I not study that? I blew it. I could have had a much higher grade if I had studied. I was too lazy!" But thinking thoughts such as these wastes precious seconds that one could be using on another question. These thoughts also tend to create negative emotions that distract from the next task.

So you need to rehearse before the test, that if there is something you do not know, you will calmly take your best guess and then move on to the next question without fretting at all about the

previous one. If anything else unwanted happens, you take it in stride and concentrate on getting the next question right. This advice is overridden if you need to help put out a fire, resuscitate a fellow test-taker, pull yourself out of the rubble of an earthquake, and so forth. But for the more ordinary bad things, you don't have time to worry about them!

The author advises

A. preparing so thoroughly that you know the answers to all the questions,

or

B. preparing not to distress yourself when you don't know the answer to a question or when other bad things happen?

161. While the test timer is running, you don't have time for the types of thoughts I've called awfulizing, getting down on yourself, and blaming someone else. You need to spend your time loading test questions into your memory, processing the question, and outputting answers. You do have time, however, for some

celebration. You should take a split second to say "Yay!" or something synonymous very often when you think you've gotten an answer right. Internal celebration energizes you and reinforces you for the effort you are putting out.

The author advises

A. avoiding all emotion while taking a test,
or
B. avoiding the thoughts that produce painful emotion, but doing the sort of celebration that reinforces and energizes you?

Relaxation, Meditation, and Biofeedback

162. The next guideline is to use relaxation, meditation, and/or biofeedback to practice lowering your level of arousal and increasing your sense of focus.

One technique I recommend may be called "breathing and relaxing the muscles." You sit and close your eyes, and pay attention to the rhythm of your breathing. Each time you breathe out, you try to get some of your muscles more

relaxed. So the rhythm is "breathe in ... relax out." If your attention wanders from this, and you find yourself thinking about something else, you don't get down on yourself, but simply bring your attention back to the muscle relaxation in rhythm with the breathing.

The more you practice this, the more you will be able to bring your level of excitement down, whenever you want to (including just before or during a test) simply by relaxing your muscles. A brief practice session close to every day in relaxing in this way will be useful for most people.

This section advises that you use the breathing and relaxing the muscles technique

A. only when you need it, such as when you feel anxious during a test,
or
B. in frequent practice sessions, regularly, outside of test situations?

163. Many people look at relaxation techniques as

something to be used only in moments of anxiety, in the same way that you would use a pain pill only when you are feeling pain. This strategy doesn't work well. What does work well is to practice frequently, gradually cultivating more and more skill in the art of achieving relaxed focus.

If you use any technique only when you are scared, that technique is likely to become associated with fear, so that after a while, using it when you are not scared would tend to bring up feelings of fear! On the other hand, if you use it many times when you are not particularly scared and achieve a feeling of calm focus, the technique becomes more and more associated, over time, with those calm focused feelings.

This section gives a reason why

A. you should practice relaxation techniques frequently, not just on an "as needed" basis,
or
B. you should explore several different techniques of

relaxation/meditation, and pick the one that works best for you?

164. As you practice relaxation or meditation, it's often fun and interesting to add biofeedback. With biofeedback, you use a gadget to measure something about what your body is doing, so that you can get feedback on what your relaxation strategies are doing. I've found three types of feedback most valuable. First is skin conductance level: as you get more relaxed, your fingertips sweat less, and skin conductance goes down. Second is fingertip temperature: as you get more relaxed, your fingertip temperature rises. And third is muscle tension: as you get more relaxed, your muscle tension goes down. It's fun to play around with the machines that measure these things, and to learn to make these different measures go up and down at will. The more control you gain over your body's level of arousal, the more you will find yourself automatically adjusting it so as to get peak performance.

The author feels that when you have practiced biofeedback a lot, you can adjust your level of arousal to get peak performance

A. only when you are consciously thinking about it,
or
B. automatically, that is without consciously paying attention to every little adjustment?

Blunder Control

165. There is more to achieving peak performance on tests than controlling anxiety. Even someone who is at the ideal level of arousal can make costly blunders on tests, particularly science and math tests. How do you reduce them? Checking your work is one traditional way. But many test-takers do well to finish a test, and it's out of the question to go over every question a second time for checking.

The strategy I recommend, after you've gotten fast enough at answering questions that you have some time for checking, is to check each problem immediately after solving it. In complicated

multi-step problems, I recommend checking each step immediately after carrying it out.

The strategy the author recommends is

A to finish all the questions before doing any checking, and then go back and check the ones that you are uncertain about,
or
B. to check each question or step as you do it?

166. Why do I recommend this strategy? Because if you finish all questions and then go back to check, you will spend lots of time rereading questions, re-loading the question into your memory. But if you check while the question is still in memory, you can save lots of time. The checking can be very fast.

Why do I recommend quickly checking after every step of a multi-step problem? Because if you make a blunder early on, all your work after that will be wasted. By catching blunders early in the process, you can save yourself the frustration of having to go through all the steps over again.

The purpose of this section was to

A. explain why checking as you go along is a good strategy,
or
B. describe exactly how you check?

167. If you are going to check as you go along, you should definitely use this strategy in your practice tests. You want to make sure that you will have time to check as you go along and still finish the test. You may need to increase the speed of your checking, if you find that you run out of time. If you can't get fast enough to check every question as you go along, you will have to figure out from practice tests how much checking to eliminate.

The author feels that

A. you should check every question as you go along, no matter how long it takes,
or

B. you should use practice tests to improve your checking speed and to figure out how much checking you should take the time for?

The Error-Reduction Checklist

168. When you check, you don't want to simply go through the same mental processes that you used in solving the problem the first time. You want to have a mental list of possible blunders, and you rapidly search for each one of them, mentally crossing it off the list if you fail to find it and correcting it if you do find it.

The list of possible blunders has been called the "error-reduction checklist." Every time you make a blunder on a practice test, you classify it. What sort of blunder was this? You make a list of every type of mistake you are likely to make, and check for the most likely ones.

The main point of this section is that

A. when you check your work, you go through a mental checklist of possible errors,

or
B. pilots and surgeons and others who do high-stakes work should also have error-reduction checklists?

169. Here's an example of an error-reduction checklist for a math student.

1. Did I copy numbers correctly?
2. Did I keep straight what each number represented?
3. Did I do all calculations accurately?
4. Did I make sure any conversions of measurement units were done right?
5. Did I make sure I answered the question that was actually asked, and not some other question that could have been asked?
6. Did I pay particular attention to crucial words in the directions the question gives? (For example, did I notice the word *not* in the question "Which of the following is *not* true?")
7. Does the answer make sense, estimating from the original question?

8. Once I found the answer, did I enter it correctly on the answer sheet?

Of course, the error reduction checklist you will want to use depends on what types of questions you are answering, and what sorts of mistakes you make if you're not careful.

The author believes that

A. the error-reduction checklist you just read is the one you should use on all tests,
or
B. you should make your own error-reduction checklist, listing the types of errors you have made on practice tests?

Adjusting the Frequency of Review, To Fit Your Own Forgetting Curve

170. This chapter gives ideas that are perhaps more overlooked and neglected than any others in this book. Yet they are extremely important – indeed, they can make the difference between a smashing success and a dreadful failure. The major idea of this chapter has to do with discovering for yourself how frequently you need to review the important information and skills you need to remember. How often you need to review depends upon your own "forgetting curve": how fast you forget a certain type of information or skill if you do not review. The faster you tend to forget, the more often you need to review.

The main idea of this section is that

A. you should trust your instructor, and complete review exercises whenever they are assigned,
or

B. you should figure out how often you need to review to keep yourself from forgetting important information and skills?

171. Often textbooks and courses seem to be based on what we can call the "no forgetting story": once a student learns something, the student never forgets it. Imagine a science course. The student studies one chapter, takes a test on it, and goes on to the next chapter. At the end of the course, the student has learned all the chapters and all the material is mastered, according to this story.

But what happens more often goes according to the "forgetting without review story." The student studies one chapter, and takes a test on it. Then, while studying the second chapter, the student forgets a great deal of the first chapter. While studying the third chapter, the student forgets even more of the first chapter and forgets a great deal of the second chapter. By the time the student has finished the tenth chapter, the first nine chapters have nearly vanished from memory.

The unpleasant picture the author paints is that

A. as the student learns one bit of information in school, the student is forgetting many of the previous bits,
or
B. the student is remembering all the information, but does not know how to apply it?

172. The "forgetting without review" story is very unpleasant. If you are enacting it, you are working very hard to load lots of information into your memory. At the end of a course, almost all that effort has nothing to show for it! This is the very opposite of the effort-payoff connection. It is quite discouraging. And yet, according to my observation, it goes on very frequently. It's one of the main things that make education frustrating and depressing for many people.

The major point of this section is that

A. if you pay more attention to how your effort gets you better results, you can increase the effort-payoff connection,
or
B. the experience of forgetting the previous material while you are learning the present material can make academic work very unpleasant?

173. Let's give another example of the "forgetting without review" story. A student takes piano lessons. The student learns to play a song. When the student can play the song fairly well, the teacher moves on to a new song. This continues for a couple of years, after which time they have covered 20 songs. Someone proposes that the student give a concert of all those 20 songs. But the student cannot play 20 songs – the student can only play one song! And even that song is not played expertly, but only fairly well. Why? Because while learning each new song, the student has been forgetting all the previous ones! The student and the teacher have invested many hours of effort, and all they have

to show for it is a repertoire of one song!

The purpose of this section is

A. to make the point that one can take many piano lessons without building up a good repertoire of songs,
or
B. to give another example of the frustration that occurs with the "forgetting without review" story?

174. Suppose the science student in our first example takes a final exam after studying a couple of days. The student manages to cram in enough to get 55% correct. The student fails the course. Other people think, "That student isn't very smart," and the student thinks the same.

Suppose someone asks the piano student to play a random selection of the 20 songs she has studied. The student bravely attempts them, making lots of mistakes and hesitations and sounding terrible. The person thinks, "This student has no talent," and the student thinks the same thing.

This section is meant to illustrate that

A. some people have higher IQ's than others,
or
B. the end of the "forgetting without review" story is often that the student and other people think that the student is stupid or without talent?

175. What is often the case is not that the student is stupid or without talent, but that the student has a *forgetting curve that is too steep relative to the review schedule.*

Let's think about the meaning of what we've just said. What is the forgetting curve? Let's imagine that someone memorizes some facts, so that the person can remember 100% of them. One day later, the person can remember 90% of them. Two days later, the person can remember 70% of them. Seven days after learning, the person can only remember 20% of them. Ten days after learning, the person can only remember 5% of them. Suppose you were to plot these numbers on a graph, with days after first learning on the horizontal axis and percent remembered on the vertical axis.

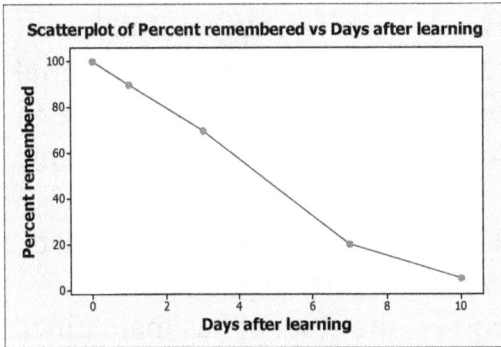

Scatterplot of Percent remembered vs Days after learning

The "steepness" of this forgetting curve is how fast it goes downhill as you go from left to right. The student in this sample is forgetting fairly quickly. The student's memory of the facts is almost entirely gone after 10 days. If a second student remembered 90% after 10 days, and still remembered 80% after 30 days, that student would have a much less steep forgetting curve.

Saying that someone has a steeper forgetting curve than someone else is saying that

A. the person can't learn as well, or
B. the person forgets faster?

176. Now let's replace the "forgetting without review" story with another one, in which people "adjust the review schedule to fit their forgetting curve."

Our science student studies Chapter 1. While doing so, he makes a list of questions and answers on this chapter. He can go through the questions quickly and say the answers. Then he starts studying Chapter 2. But the very first day he starts Chapter 2, he skims Chapter 1 quickly, rereading any paragraphs that he feels shaky on, and then he quickly goes through his list of questions and supplies the answers. Because his forgetting curve has only gone down a little bit, it doesn't take long for him to bump it back up again. He is now back up to 100%.

He reviews Chapter 1 several times while studying Chapter 2. While studying Chapter 3, he reviews both Chapters 1 and 2. While studying Chapter 4, he also reviews Chapters 1, 2, and 3. He does all this in about 20 minutes of review every day.

This section tells a story in which

A. the student reviews each past chapter of his text, while learning each present chapter, reviewing about 20 minutes every day,
or
B. the student does a review every two months?

177. How does the student do this review in 20 minutes a day, as more and more chapters get added to the review agenda? He finds that after he has reviewed a chapter many times, all he has to do is to glance at it quickly just to check that the material is still in his mind. He finds that he can look down his list of questions and supply the correct answers with great speed. The process of review with a given chapter gets faster and faster the more he does it. He also finds that when the same material has been reviewed a certain number of times, the forgetting curve doesn't go down as steeply. Thus after he's reviewed Chapter 1 five times, he only needs to look at it once every week rather than once a day to keep it in memory.

This section explains

A. how to review different subjects,
or
B. why you can successfully review as more and more material piles up, without having to spend lots and lots more time reviewing?

178. The end of this story is that when the final examination comes, the student has maintained all the previous material in memory, and the student does so well on the final exam that people say, "You're lucky to be so smart in science." This, we'll remember, was the same student, with the same forgetting curve, who would have been called stupid in science; the difference was a carefully adjusted schedule of reviewing. The student spent 20 minutes a day reviewing that he otherwise might have spent on video games.

The point of this section is that

A. it's important not to waste time on video games,
or

B. a carefully constructed review schedule can make the difference between success and failure?

179. Let's tell the story of "adjusting the review schedule to fit the forgetting curve" again. Let's imagine our piano student. She learns song number 1, and starts song number 2. But while she's working on song 2, she takes a few minutes every day to practice song 1. While learning song 2, she actually gets *more* skilled at song 1. While learning song 3, she takes some time each day to practice both song 1 and song 2.

After this continues for a while, she finds that she doesn't have to practice songs 1 and 2 every day. She finds that if she practices them only every five days, they come back to memory. Then she finds that they continue to come back if she practices them every 10 days. The review every 10 days has the same feeling of "bumping the forgetting curve up from 95% to 100%" that the review every day formerly had. Still later, she is able to bump songs 1 and 2 up to 100% by practicing them every 20 days.

Meanwhile, with each new song she takes on, she continues practicing the previous ones. This review takes her about 15 minutes a day. When someone asks her to play several songs from her repertoire, she can deliver, on the spot, a concert with any of 20 songs played expertly. The person who is listening says, "You are so lucky to have such musical talent!"

In this "adjusting the review schedule" story as well as the previous one,

A. a few minutes of systematic review each day made the difference between being thought of as "talented" or "untalented," or
B. the amount of review necessary to do each day was 20 times as much to keep 20 songs in the repertoire as it was to keep 1 song in the repertoire?

180. How do you know how much to review, and how often to review? There is no fixed frequency or amount of time that is best for all people, since people forget at much different rates.

Even within one person, the rates of forgetting are different for different subject matters. For example, one person may find that math theorems stick in the mind almost permanently, whereas spelling words need to be reviewed very frequently; someone else may find just the opposite pattern.

The point of this section is that

A. 15 to 20 minutes of review per day per subject will work wonders,
or
B. the amount of review needs to be individualized not only for each person, but also for each subject for a given person?

181. There are ways to tell if you are reviewing frequently enough, however. You should feel as though the ideas, facts, or skills you went over before are coming back quickly. If you feel that you are learning them all over again from the beginning, then you have waited too long to review, and your next review should be a good bit sooner. You should feel that you remember almost all of what

you learned before – that most of your review is bringing things back to mind, rather than relearning them. If you are answering practice questions during your review, you should be able to answer them quickly.

A way of summarizing this section is

A. if during your review you have to go slowly and do a lot of relearning, you should review more frequently,
or
B. to use the technique of "flash review," you look at a page of your text and let the main ideas on that page flash across your mind quickly?

182. A point I've made several times in this book is worth making again here. Don't get into the typical student mind-set that it's out of the question to do any work that is not assigned by your teacher. Your teacher does not know the shape of your individual forgetting curve! Any classroom teacher can only assign review according to a best guess of what the average student will require.

Even if you have an individual tutor, the tutor may not consider it his or her job to get you to go back and review the material you have already covered. The person who is best positioned to know how often you need to review is YOU. If you can muster the self-discipline to figure out a good review schedule for yourself and put it into effect, you will have taken a massive step toward ensuring your success as a student.

The author, in this section, is attempting to

A. make teachers take more responsibility for figuring out students' review schedules,
or
B. give you the responsibility to figure out and enact the best review schedule for yourself?

The Importance of Sleep and Circadian Rhythms

183. This is a chapter where it takes very little time to say what should be done. But it takes a great deal of self-discipline to do what should be done. Of many students, very few of them can actually carry out the advice in this chapter.

There are two pieces of advice. First, get enough sleep. Second, get sleep in a steady rhythm, wherein you go to bed and get up at close to the same time each day.

The main advice in this section is

A. get enough exercise so that you'll be able to sleep,
or
B. get enough sleep, and get it in a steady rhythm (meaning a consistent bedtime and time of awakening)?

184. Why is it important to get enough sleep? One reason is given by recent research showing that sleep is important for "consolidating" memories. This means that with adequate sleep, our memories are able to stick with us longer, rather than slipping into oblivion. In a previous chapter we spoke of the forgetting curve; getting adequate sleep probably alters the forgetting curve, making it not slope so steeply!

The main point of this section is that

A. enough sleep helps you not to forget so quickly,
or
B. if you learn relaxation techniques, you will be able to sleep more easily?

185. How much sleep is enough? Richard Ferber, an expert on sleep problems, reports that on the average, sleep requirements decrease as children get older, but not very quickly and not to very low levels. Five year olds do best with 11 hours of sleep a day; 9 year olds with 10 hours; 14 year

olds with 9 hours; and 18 year olds, with 8 ¼ hours. The sleep needs for ages in between those give are between the hours given. So, since a 12 year old is about half way between 9 and 14, you'd guess that the sleep recommendation would be about half way between 9 and 10, or 9.5 hours.

According to these recommendations, a 13 year old who goes to sleep at 11:30 and gets up at 6:00 is getting

A. half an hour less than recommended,
or
B. around two and a half hours less than recommended?

186. Surveys confirm that children, adolescents, and adults on the average seem to get less sleep than the body was built for. Probably one culprit responsible for this fact is the revolution in electronic inventions, the most important of which was the electric light bulb. The late-night availability of television, the Internet, peers with cell phones to talk and text with, and so forth, combine to provide all sorts of tempting activities to do late at night. Add to this the cultural custom of parties and face-to-face socializing that goes on during late night (and early morning) hours, and you have a massive epidemic of insufficient sleep, particularly among young people.

In this section the author

A. tells you how to get adequate sleep,
or
B. speculates on why inadequate sleep is rampant among young people in our culture?

187. Different people do vary in their sleep requirements. Some adults, for example, seem to do well on as little as 6 hours of sleep per night, while some seem to need 10 hours for adequate functioning. Each person must experiment to find how much sleep is enough. As you are experimenting, if you find yourself dozing off to sleep in class, or while having a conversation, or every time you

ride in a car, that's a pretty obvious sign you're not getting enough sleep. People who avoid falling asleep during daytime activities only with caffeine or other drugs also should try drastically increasing their nighttime sleep.

But more subtly, you should see how fast you learn, how well you remember, and how efficiently you can work problems and organize your writing with various amounts of sleep. If your mind is more efficient with more sleep, notice that and act upon your findings!

The purpose of this section was to

A. help you figure out how much sleep is best for you,
or
B. help you find ways to get to sleep earlier?

188. In addition to getting enough sleep, it's very useful to keep up a steady sleep rhythm, which means going to bed and getting up at close to the same time each day. Why is this important? Because there's a clock-like mechanism inside our brains that keeps track of when it's time to go to sleep and when it's time to be awake. This clock sends messages by various hormones that tell our bodies how alert to be. Our minds work best when our clocks are telling us, "You're supposed to be awake and alert now!"

Many school kids spend the first couple of periods of a school day with their bodies' really thinking they should be asleep. They are very inefficient at these times. Many of these students have a hard time getting to sleep at night, but have a hard time getting out of bed in the morning; these students usually have their clocks set too late. They need to reset the clocks so that they get sleepy earlier and wake up earlier. Food, bright light, and exercise first thing in the morning tend to set the clock earlier; the same things late at night tend to set the clock later.

The problem this section referred to was that students

A. have their clocks that influence sleeping set too late,

or
B. have their clocks that influence sleeping set too early?

189. The rhythm of sleeping and waking is referred to as a circadian rhythm. The word *circadian* means "about daily" – it means that it takes about one day for the cycle to start over.

It is much easier to set the time of sleeping and waking later than to set it earlier. This fact causes a big problem for students who tend to stay up late and get up late on week ends. On week ends, the clock gets set later, and the week days are not sufficient to get it set back. As a result, millions of students go to sleep too late on week days and get up a long time before they have had enough sleep. They build up a sleep debt during the week days, and treat their exhaustion by sleeping very late during the week ends. The problem thus keeps going. The result is impaired mental efficiency.

The main idea of this section is that

A. getting exercise first thing in the morning is important for anyone who wants to set the sleep rhythm earlier,
or
B. sleeping late and staying up late on week ends contribute to the sleep rhythm problems many students have?

190. What are students to do about the fact that so many fun social activities take place very late at night? One solution to this problem is to keep the waking time in the morning steady even after a late night, and to make up for lost sleep with an early afternoon nap. A different solution is to make such good friends and to become so socially skilled that you can do all the fun socializing you want to on your own terms, during the hours before your regular bedtime occurs.

This section mentioned two

A. reasons why you should keep your time of awakening steady, even if you can't keep your bedtime steady,

or

B. possible ways of solving the
problem of fun social activities
that occur late at night?

Ways of Making Academic Work Into A Social Activity

191. Parents have discovered that when a child is doing bad things, it's a fairly effective punishment to make the child stay in a room by himself for a few minutes. This method of punishment is called time-out. Why does it work? Because people are social animals, and we like being with one another as a general rule. Most of us don't tend to like staying in rooms by ourselves for long periods of time.

I think that this fact is one of the main reasons why some students can't get themselves to do enough academic work: such work requires that they go into a room and be alone.

The temptation to be with other people is just too strong. So they come out from their rooms and talk with people, or watch people talking on television, or interact with imaginary people on video games, or try to provoke their sibling to chase them – anything but shutting oneself up alone.

The main point the author makes in this section is that

A. if you want to study best, don't do it where you are distracted by other people's talking,
or
B. having to be alone while studying is one of the main reasons that many students don't study enough?

192. If it's not much fun for you to study alone, it makes sense to make a social activity out of studying. The more good social pleasure you can get while doing academic work, the more you will be reinforced, or rewarded, for doing it. The more pleasant you can make your academic work, the more you will wind up doing.

This chapter will address the question, how do you make academic work a social activity, but still get a lot accomplished?

The author sets the stage that in this chapter,

A. we'll think about ways to enjoy being alone more,
or
B. we'll think about ways to make academic work into a pleasant social activity?

193. When we try to make academic work a social activity, the temptation is to get one or more friends together for a work party, but to spend the entire time talking with each other and goofing off. When you arrange a work party, make sure that the other person understands that you really do want to get some work done. And be sure to pick the type of person who has the self-discipline to get work done with you.

This section has to do with

A. whether human beings are really "social animals,"
or
B. avoiding planning work parties which turn into parties without any work?

194. One of the simplest and best ways to plan a work party is just to plan a schedule of sitting and working together, alternating with walking and talking with each other. For example, we sit and work for 50 minutes, and then we walk and talk for 10 minutes. Then we start the cycle over again. By getting in some socializing and exercise, we recharge our batteries for another period of time where we're going to be more solitary and still.

This works even better if each time that we take a break, we share with each other what we've accomplished during the last work period. We support and reinforce each other for what we've accomplished. We are in a "cooperative game," where we are each trying to help the other feel good about being productive.

A summary of this section is that

A. you and a friend can alternate periods of work with periods of walking, talking, and celebrating your accomplishments,
or
B. it's better to have a work party with just one other person rather than a whole group?

195. Here's a second plan for making work a social activity. If you are both studying the same textbook or other book, you can just take turns reading it aloud to one another. You can switch after each paragraph, each page, or each section. If, as in this book, answering these questions and celebrating right answers gives more opportunity for some positive interaction and mutual encouragement. Any time you want to discuss what you have read, you say whatever you want. However, you might need to resist the temptation to stray too far from the topic, if you really want to study.

One of the advantages of this method is that the practice reading aloud helps with the skills of both reading and public speaking.

The technique the author describes in this section may be called

A. taking turns reading aloud,
or
B. making up questions and answers together?

196. Here's the third technique, for those who are working on the same material. You read each paragraph, either aloud or silently, and then one of you does (aloud) a "reflection" of what the paragraph says – in other words, you summarize what the paragraph was trying to get across. Then you read the next paragraph, and it's the other person's turn. You can celebrate particularly good reflections that the other person makes, or give your own reflections if you think it would be helpful for the other to hear a different version.

The technique of this section could be called

A. using flash cards with one another,
or
B. taking turns doing the reflections exercise with each paragraph?

197. Here's the fourth technique of socializing while working. One person is the secretary, and sits at the computer. You both read the

material you are working on. As soon as one of you reads something that could be turned into a good question, you speak up and raise the question. The secretary writes down the question. Someone else, or perhaps the person who raised the question, speaks out the answer to the question. The secretary writes down the answer to the question. When you are done, you can read the questions and let people take turns giving the answers.

This technique can be called

A. reading aloud to one another, or
B. making a quiz and answering it together?

198. Here's the fifth technique of socializing while working together. For math, chemistry, physics, or any other problem-solving subject, you simply sit together and do problems together. You can do each problem together and compare results.

If one person is shakier at the problem-solving techniques than the other, that person can solve the problems while the other person plays the following cooperative game: the more skilled person tries to give hints that help the other person solve the problems with as much pleasure and as little frustration as possible, while taking away as little as possible of the other person's pleasure from discovery. In other words, you give just enough hints for the other to have smooth sailing, but not so many hints that the other feels you are doing the work for him.

After you've finished a set of problems, if there's a set of answers, you check your answers with them. (When my daughter and I do this, one of us sings the answers from the list in the book, while the other checks those on our papers.) You celebrate the answers the two of you cooperatively got right, and you learn from the ones you got wrong.

This technique can be called

A. doing problems together, either independently or with one giving hints to the other,

or

B. doing problems together to see who can get the most right?

199. Here's a sixth technique. In this, you both read the same material silently together. Then, you take some time and "have a seminar." This means that you discuss the ideas you have read. But you don't just recite them back. You question any of the ideas you disagree with. You tell ideas that you think are consequences of the ideas you read. You comment on what the significance is of the ideas you've taken in, and how they can be used. You comment on how these ideas fit together or clash with other ideas you've heard of. You think of questions about related topics that are stimulated by what you've read, questions the subject matter stimulates, not just questions asking someone to remember the subject matter. You get ideas for research studies someone could do to shed more light on the topic raised. In other words, you say as smart things about what you've read as you possibly can, playing the cooperative game of helping both you and your comrade have as much fun with the "life of the mind" as you possibly can.

This technique is best called

A. rapid review

or

B. having a seminar?

200. Here's the last technique of this chapter. This involves doing time trials together. If there is something you want to get very fast and fluent at, you get a stopwatch or a watch with a second hand, and a calculator, and whatever else you need. One person, for example, calls out the answers to math facts as fast as possible, while the second checks to see if the answers are correct and stops the other after one minute. Then it's time for the second trial, either with the first person going again or with the second person taking a turn.

Or, the two people go through the questions and answers over a chapter of information, and they time themselves on how quickly and accurately they can answer the questions.

I like for these activities to be cooperative rather than competitive games. That is, it doesn't matter if one person is faster than the other – what matters is that both people improve their times the more trials they do.

The technique in this section can be called

A. the reflections exercise,
or
B. doing time trials with each other?

Avoid the Most Common Time-Wasters

201. Where can you find the time to do the things suggested in this book? I've advised breaking out of the mind-set that says that when you are done with what your teacher assigns, your schoolwork is finished. I've said that some of your most productive, valuable, and rewarding work is self-assigned, not assigned by a teacher. But doing self-assigned work takes time.

There is a sad fact, which I think of as my first law of time management: if you start doing more of something regularly, you have to stop doing so much of something else. You can't just get a gift from heaven of more hours in a day.

A summary of this section is that

A. self-assigned tasks take time, and if you do more of them, you have to do less of something else, or
B. very few students can do self-assigned work?

202. What can you do less of, to make time for more self-assigned academic work? For the average U.S. student, there is one time waster that stands head and shoulders above all others: television. Some surveys reveal that U.S. students devote about four hours a day, seven days a week, to watching television. If even a quarter of this time could be diverted to self-assigned academic work, the effect on students' success could be enormous.

A summary of this section is that

A. the habit of self-assigning academic work gets easier the more you do it,
or
B. for the average student, time for self-assigned academic work can come from watching less television?

203. Even though for the average U.S. student, television is the biggest time waster, for many

others, other electronic technologies have taken the place of television. Many spend huge amounts of time on video games, including online games, and on surfing the Internet. Some spend lots of time on getting and listening to music.

This section says that

A. video games, the Internet, and music can be big time wasters for some,
or
B. electronic technology has become much faster over the last several years?

204. Texting friends and talking with friends by phone, and connecting with friends by social networking sites such as Facebook can be a very useful and satisfying activity. If one puts some thought into the words one is sending or saying to someone else, the experience can be very beneficial in developing the essential skill of communicating in words.

However, there is a downside to these activities. First, for some people they can become excessive. Second, many students get into the habit of letting themselves be interrupted in the middle of whatever they are doing, whenever they get a message from anyone else. This habit is the opposite of the sort of sustained concentration on one thing that makes for academic success. Thus: when you are concentrating on your academic work, you need to turn off any pop-up messaging systems and turn off the volume of any phone. You need to insulate yourself from people who want to contact you, at least for a while.

The author's attitude toward electronic socializing is that

A. you should avoid it altogether,
or
B. it can be good, but you have to set limits on it and particularly not let it interrupt you?

205. Sports are for many students a major time-waster.
Many students believe that it is more important and much more exciting to become a sports star

than an academic star. And the structure of U.S. education encourages this idea. If you walk into the lobby of a high school, you are more likely to find athletic trophies than academic trophies. When people speak of "school spirit," they think of the football team, not the math team or debate team. In major colleges, athletic teams often have huge budgets, and football coaches can be paid more than the presidents of colleges. Colleges are willing to give scholarships for the sake of winning teams. Crowds of people may scream and cheer when you score in basketball, but you are likely to go through a lifetime without hearing one scream about your solving a math problem.

But the fact that our culture pays so much attention to sports does not change the fact that after graduation from the educational system into the real world of earning a living, the sports skills one has spent countless hours practicing are almost always worth very little. By contrast, academic skills give the key to job success.

The major point of this section is that

A. many sports encourage aggression and cause injury, or
B. despite the emphasis that schools give to sports, academic skills lead to much greater success in earning a living?

206. Many U.S. students I have known have become involved in many extracurricular activities, no one of which could be considered a time-waster. They are all worthwhile and potentially fun. But when the extracurricular activities crowd out the time for the student's main job, which is to become expert at reading, writing, math, and science, the extracurricular activities can become very harmful.

Would you like to participate in a team sport, plus martial arts, plus a musical instrument, plus debate team, plus dance, the school play, and a few clubs? A few students proudly put all this on their resumes, along with top grades and test scores. Some enjoy the hectic lifestyle involved in such multitasking; others secretly hate it. But many, many others find that such activities keep them from doing their main job, i.e. academics, well enough to enjoy it.

The author's attitude is that

A. college admissions folks like to see lots of extracurricular activities, so you should do as many as you can,
or
B. don't do so many extracurricular activities that you don't have time for your main job?

207. One of the *least* time-wasting activities a student can do, in my opinion, is tutoring other students. Tutoring helps you use your academic skills not just to get high grades, but to help other human beings. Being of service to others is greatly underemphasized in education, at the expense of "becoming a star." Tutoring also gives practice in crucial work skills such as keeping appointments, and it reinforces your own knowledge of the subjects you are teaching. If you are good enough at tutoring, you can earn money that people consider some of the best dollars they have ever spent.

A summary of this section is that

A. for several different reasons, tutoring other students is a very productive use of time,
or
B. before you can tutor others, you need to get your own skills in top condition?

208. You may find it very instructive to keep a time log, not as a regular practice, but for a while. To do this, you write down the time whenever you start a new activity. You keep records that allow you to answer the question, how much time are you devoting to homework? How much to self-assigned academic work? How much to various different subjects? How much to TV, video games, electronic socializing, sports, and so forth? The more you can consciously decide, where am I wasting too much time, what do I want to do less,

the more time you will have
available for high-priority
activities.

The point of this section is

A. it helps to keep records, for a
while, of where your time goes, to
help you decide consciously how
to spend your time,
or
B. one of the most important time-
management techniques is to
make a daily to-do list?

Steps Toward Becoming an Independent Scholar

209. What does it mean to be an independent scholar? It means that if you need to learn something, you can usually figure out a way to teach yourself. When you need people to help you, you can find those people and use their help to the fullest. You don't need someone threatening you with a bad grade to make you do your work. You don't need a bunch of other people working alongside you to make you work. You are driven by goals, and not just short-term goals. You can work toward things that happen months or years from now, and take pleasure in the fact that you are making progress. You can "self-assign" tasks rather than needing someone to be your taskmaster. You can feel good about the progress you make, even when it has not born fruit yet.

If you can do these things, you are hugely more likely to achieve your goals.

In this section the author describes

A. why some people fail at becoming an independent scholar, or
B. what it means to be an independent scholar?

210. A very important step to becoming an independent scholar comes when someone sits with you and teaches you something, and you realize that the person is doing something nice for you. You don't resist the person, but you cooperate with him or her. You are letting the person help you with the "meet the challenge game," and you are avoiding the temptation to play the "frustrate the authority" game.

Although it may seem strange, one of the most important steps toward becoming an independent scholar is accepting help in a cooperative way.

The author believes that

A. cooperating with a helper is a very important step toward becoming an independent scholar,

or

B. if you want to be independent, you need to reject all help?

211. Another big step comes when you work, not just when your teacher or helper is watching over your shoulder, but when you are on your own. In other words, you do homework. If you are able to do homework at home (as contrasted to doing homework for the next class while the previous class is going on) this step counts for even more.

In this section the author makes the point that

A. homework causes a lot of conflict between parents and children,
or
B. doing homework is a big step toward becoming an independent learner?

212. At some point you ask yourself not just "What is due tomorrow," but "What is my complete to do list, and how do I want to schedule the tasks?" You are able to start on projects that come weeks from now far ahead of time, without waiting until the last moment.

The skill this section discusses is

A. self-reinforcement,
or
B. planning ahead and not procrastinating?

213. A big breakthrough comes when you work on academic tasks that no one has assigned you – projects that you have assigned to yourself. This represents breaking out of the passive mind-set – disputing the idea that "I never do any academic work unless I have to." Perhaps you read a textbook other than the one you are assigned. Perhaps you take practice tests to prepare for a test you will take two years from now. Perhaps you realize you are shaky on a component skill for the more complex skill you're working on now, and you go down the hierarchy of difficulty to easier subject matter and work your way back up. Maybe you do speed drills on something that is slowing you down. Perhaps you read or

write or solve problems just because you are interested in the subject.

The skill promoted in this section was

A. turning in your homework,
or
B. self-assigning tasks you don't have to do for school?

214. You learn how to make self-assigned tasks pay off for you. You write things that people like to read, and you take pleasure from that. You produce works that do people good. You use your skills to help yourself. You enter contests. You teach other students. You simply enjoy what you are doing as an end in itself. Or, you reward yourself in your own mind for getting more and more skilled, knowing that the skills you are developing will pay off in known or unknown ways in the future.

This section is about

A. making self-assigned tasks rewarding for you,

or
B. knowing how to work without getting any reward, either from others or from yourself?

215. While doing your self-assigned projects, feeling good about your progress usually means that you are repeatedly measuring your progress. You test yourself, then work and learn, then test yourself again, and continue until you have accomplished your goal. Then you continue working to maintain it.

How do you monitor your progress? You time yourself on any of the tasks mentioned in the chapter on The Need for Speed, or any other academic tasks. You give yourself practice tests, or sign up for real tests. You keep track of your scores on the achievement tests you take at school. You keep a portfolio of your writing, and notice how it gets better and better. You rate on a scale of 10 how pleasant it is to get your homework done. You count the number of pages or chapters you've written on your book. You keep track of how well you placed in the math contest. Or you use any other way of measuring your progress that you can think of.

The main suggestion in this section was to

A. not waste time, but keep on doing things that accomplish something,
or
B. keep track of how much you are accomplishing and how much you are improving?

216. Suppose you get to the stage where you can do all the following things: You carefully choose your most important goals, self-assign the tasks necessary to reach them, keep track of your progress along the way, adjust your work strategies so as to keep the progress coming fast enough, and feel good about every bit of progress, without needing someone else to compel you to do all these things. Then you have not only become an independent scholar; you have learned habits that will help you to reach each of your life's goals!

The purposes of this section were to

A. summarize what is meant by being an independent scholar, and link independent scholarship skills to other life goals,
or
B. explain the reasons why so many people fail to become independent scholars?

Learning Spelling

217. If this book were written in Esperanto, and everyone spoke this language, this chapter could be eliminated. Esperanto was made up specifically to be easy to learn, and there is a one-to-one correspondence between the letters and the sounds they make. If you can pronounce a word, you simply write down the sounds in that word and you have correctly spelled it. Even in Spanish, this is largely true. But English is a different story. There are many words that you have to simply memorize.

The point of this section is that

A. English has enough exceptions to the rules of correspondence between letters and sounds that you have to do a lot of memorizing to learn to spell well, or
B. Esperanto is a language that was constructed to try to produce international cooperation?

218. I heard a story of a very bright young girl who burst into tears when she first found out that the word *once* was spelled o-n-c-e. Her tears came from the realization that her language didn't always follow the rules she had learned so far for what sounds the letters make. She grasped in an instant her future fate of spending many hours memorizing letter combinations. *Once*, in a logical system of spelling, should be spelled w-u-n-s.

The point of this story is

A. to argue that people should push for a different spelling of the word *once*,
or
B. to dramatize the point that many English words don't follow regular rules of sounds for letters?

219. To give another example of why English spelling is not easy, think about words with an el sound at the end. Some are spelled

with an al, such as brutal, general, legal, and signal. Some are spelled with an el, such as novel, shovel, travel, and label. And many others are spelled with an le, such as bottle, ankle, circle, and handle. There is no rule that you can memorize that tells you when to use which. You simply have to memorize each word.

Here's another example. Lots of words have an *er* sound at the end. Some make this sound with er, such as writer, farmer, manager, or laborer. Others make the sound with or, such as actor, author, collector, and editor. Again, there's no rule. You just have to learn each word, separately.

The author's point in this section is that

A. by learning a few simple rules, you can improve your spelling drastically,
or
B. for many English words, there is no rule, and you simply have to memorize the spelling of the individual word?

220. There are, however, some rules that you can learn that will greatly help. Here's an example. Suppose you are adding *ing* or *ed* to a word that ends in a consonant preceded by a single vowel. When do you double that final consonant, and when do you leave it single?

For example, admit becomes admitted or admitting. Control becomes controlled or controlling. Rebel becomes rebelled or rebelling. In each of these cases we double the last consonant.

But: focus becomes focused or focusing. We don't double the s. Benefit becomes benefited or benefiting. Travel becomes traveled or traveling. No doubling in these words.

What's the difference? Actually there's a rule. In the first set of words, the last syllable gets the accent, or emphasis, when you pronounce the word. In the second set, some other syllable is accented. The rule is that you double when the last syllable is accented.

Let's try it out with commit and vomit. Since commit has the last syllable accented, we would write committed or committing. Since vomit has the first syllable accented, we would write vomited or vomiting. It works!

This section illustrates that

A. you have to memorize things like whether to double the final t in words like commit or vomit, or
B. there are some spelling rules you can learn that will reduce your need for memorizing?

221. People's brains are very different from one another when it comes to spelling. For some people spelling is much more difficult than it is for others. But spelling is a very important skill. Most jobs these days require people to write, and misspelling creates a distraction and a negative impression. What should someone do if spelling comes with great difficulty? There are two approaches: one is to label oneself as learning disabled, and to argue that one should not be held to the same standards as other people because of this disability. The other approach is

to acknowledge that learning spelling will take much longer than it does for other people, and to invest a little time each day for a long, long time, in working on this skill.

The author advises people who have learning disabilities in spelling to

A. spend a little time each day for a long time working on spelling, or
B. make sure that people honor their rights as a disabled person?

222. In becoming a good speller, the words that are more frequently used are the most important ones. In the 1950's Michael West compiled a list of about 2000 words, which was called the General Service List. About 80% of the words used in everyday speech and fairly easy writing are supposedly contained in this list. Since that time, the list has been updated by several others. There are various other attempts to arrange English words in order of how frequently they are used. A spelling textbook by Edward Fry

(entitled *Spelling Book*) is based on the 3000 most frequent words as found by a study done by American Heritage Publishing Company.

The main point of this section is that

A. the American Heritage company studied how frequently English words are used,
or
B. it makes sense to study the most frequently used English words with highest priority?

223. It is a very much achievable project to memorize the spellings of the most frequent 3000 words in English. This can be done in only one year if someone averages ten new words a day. Or it can be done in two years if one averages 10 new words every two days, and uses the other days to review the words already learned.

The main point is that

A. although it takes lots of work, learning to spell the most common 3000 English words is an achievable task,
or
B. many employers complain about the poor spelling skills of their employees?

224. I have a theory that memorizing a few new spelling words very often has an effect beyond just the words that are being memorized. When you pay attention to how words are spelled and test yourself on spelling them, you train your brain to notice how words are spelled when you read. The more your brain can notice spellings, the more you will gradually improve your spelling just by reading a lot. But it could be that for many people it requires memorizing some spelling words very often to train the brain to care about how words are spelled.

The author's theory is that

A. you can't learn to spell a word except by memorizing it from a list,
or
B. memorizing the spellings of words from a list helps your brain

to learn the spelling of other words automatically from reading?

225. Here's a strategy for studying spelling each day. The first step is picking out words that you don't already know. I think it's reasonable to start from the beginning of the General Service List or Fry's Spelling Book or any other list arranged in approximate order of difficulty. A book I wrote entitled *Manual for Tutors and Teachers of Reading* also contains words arranged in approximate order of difficulty, grouped in sets according to the phonetic principle used in the words.

There are several ways to pick out the words you don't already know how to spell. One is just to look at each word and try to decide whether you know its spelling with certainty. Another is to have someone read the words out to you and have you spell them, and to write down the ones you spell incorrectly until you have accumulated however many you want to study. The first way is the quickest; it also has the advantage that you don't rehearse

spelling the words incorrectly. The second gives the most reliable test of whether you can spell the word or not.

The purpose of this section is to

A. mention two ways of picking out words you don't already know,
or
B. explain how to visualize the letters in words while not looking at the word?

226. How important is it not to rehearse spelling words incorrectly? For example, suppose that someone tests you on a spelling word, and asks you to spell it; you take your best guess, and spell it incorrectly. The incorrect spelling that you guessed at registers in your memory, and may interfere with the memory of the correct spelling that you seek to replace it with. It could be that for some learners, the act of spelling words incorrectly interferes with their progress in spelling. As far as I know, no one has done the definitive study on how important it is not to make

unsuccessful attempts to spell words. So we don't know the answer to this question for sure.

In this section the author is referring to a possible problem resulting from

A. seeing words spelled incorrectly in other students' writing,
or
B. getting incorrect spellings into your mind from trying to spell words you don't know how to spell?

227. Researchers have studied "false memories" that people can pick up. For example, suppose someone asks a bunch of kids, "Do you remember a time when you were with your mom at a grocery store, and someone had spilled a box of eggs, and they were broken all over the floor?" The kids might all deny remembering such an event. Then, however, if they are asked again several months later, a good number of them say that they do remember such a thing happening, at a time before the first interview.

Where did this false memory come from? It probably came from the images that the children created in their minds when the interviewer asked the question the first time. Over time, they continued to remember the image, but they forgot whether it was a true event or just imaginary.

This section tries to illustrate

A. how mental images of things that didn't happen can create "false memories,"
or
B. how false memories have resulted in innocent people's being imprisoned?

228. The false memory research suggests, but does not prove, that when we are studying spelling, we should try to do it in a way that involves as few errors as possible – we should come as close as possible to "errorless learning." Thus I recommend not routinely pretesting yourself on words that you haven't studied. In other words, I recommend picking out the words you are shaky on by simply looking at them and

finding the ones you think you might have trouble on rather than having to miss them first.

This does not mean that you never test yourself on spelling. You have to test yourself very frequently to see how far you have come. But the more you can set up the conditions so that you do well on your tests, the less you run into a possible problem with false memories of spelling words.

In this section the author recommends

A. picking out words you don't already know, simply by looking at them and choosing the ones you feel shaky on,
or
B. picking out words you don't already know by having someone test you on them before you have studied them?

229. How many words should you take on in one session? You have to experiment to find out the answer to this. You want to take on few enough words that the memories of some words are not interfering with the memories of others. But you want to take on enough that you are making as rapid progress as you can. For most students, somewhere between five and twenty is usually a good number. Some researchers have suggested that as few as three words at a time may be best for some learners. You tell the number that is right for you by seeing how well you remember the words after some time has passed, and how many words you can learn to spell correctly in a week, given a certain amount of time to study spelling.

The author recommends

A. that all students work on twenty words at a time,
or
B. that students experiment to find out how many words at a time results in the largest amount of learning per week?

230. Once you have picked out a set of words to learn, what do you do? You look carefully at a word, and divide it into syllables. You notice if any letters are repeated. You notice which sounds are

made by letter combinations that you wouldn't expect. You try to see each syllable in your imagination, and you look back and make sure you visualized correctly. Then you might write the word while looking at it. You check the word carefully to see that you wrote it correctly. Then you write the word, not looking at it, and again check to make sure you spelled it correctly.

This section deals with the topic of

A. why spelling is so important, and why it's good to be able to write quickly,
or
B. how to study the words so that you'll remember how to spell them?

231.You go through this process as many times as you wish, until you are confident that you can remember the words. Then you try writing them when someone else reads them to you (or from a voice recording that you make) again. What percent did you get correct? Is that percent 100, and did you

spell them confidently, easily, and quickly, without feeling as if you were struggling or guessing? You loop through the studying process until you not only spell the words correctly one time, but also spell them fluently.

How many times does the author recommend practicing the list of words you've chosen for a session?

A. Until the first time you get them all right,
or
B. until you quickly and easily get them all correct – in other words, until you do them fluently?

232. Why do I recommend visualizing words and writing them rather than saying the letters out loud? Because most people seem to recognize misspelled words as "looking funny" rather than "sounding funny." Also, unless you're in a spelling bee, you will hardly ever be called upon to say letters out loud; every time you spell will be while writing. And finally, by writing your spelling words, either by

hand or by the keyboard, you get practice in writing skills while practicing spelling.

This section was about

A. why writing spelling words is a good practice,
or
B. why the people who want to reform and simplify English spelling are correct?

233. It's important, after learning a batch of words, to go back and review them often. As we discussed in the chapter on reviewing, you want to review them before the memory trace has decayed very much. If you bump the memory up several times before it has fallen far, you will find that you don't need to review nearly so often to keep the memory fresh. You have to experiment to find out how often to review to accommodate your own forgetting curve.

You should review the same words

A. After you have finished the entire list,
or
B. very soon after you have learned them, before you have a chance to forget?

234. Have spelling checkers made the effort of learning spelling unnecessary? Not knowing how to spell words distracts one from writing. Furthermore, spell checkers do not pick up all errors. Particularly, spell checkers cannot tell whether you are confusing homophones. Homophones are words such as their, they're, and there; two, too, and to; maid and made; that are spelled differently and mean different things despite being pronounced the same. I recommend studying a book by Leslie Presson, published by Barron's, entitled *Dictionary of Homophones*.

The following poem, put on the Internet by some unknown author, illustrates some of the limitations of spell checkers.

Learning Spelling

Ode to My Spell Checker

Eye halve a spelling checker
It came with my pea sea
It plainly marks four my revue
Miss steaks eye kin knot sea.
Eye strike a quay and type a word
And wait for it to say
Weather eye yam wrong oar write.
It shows me strait a weigh.
As soon as a mist ache is maid
It nose before two long
And eye can put the error rite.
Its rare lea ever wrong.
Eye have run this poem threw it,
I am shore your pleased too no.
Its letter perfect awl the way.
My checker told me sew.

Examples of homophones are

A. so and sew; all and awl; rite
and write;
or
B. big and large; rapid and fast;
terrible and awful?

Learning To Be A Good Writer

235. Writing is an example of a composite skill with many components. This means that if you want to write well and have the most fun writing, you need to get fluent at lots of skills that compose the skill of writing. What are those skills?

1. handwriting
2. typing (a.k.a. keyboarding)
3. spelling
4. vocabulary
5. constructing good sentences
6. using grammar well
7. using punctuation well
8. coming up with ideas about what to say that is worth saying
9. deciding which ideas fit, and don't fit, in a certain piece of writing
10. organizing ideas into a logical order
11. wording your ideas so that they communicate clearly and pleasantly to the reader
12. deciding upon the style of writing and the tone that are best for the particular purpose you're writing for
13. developing a tolerance for the processes of proofreading and revision, rather than an impatience to be done as soon as you finish the first draft
14. regulating the "internal critic" (the internal critic is your own tendency to find things wrong with your own writing) so that its action will help rather than hinder your writing

After looking at this list, would you guess that the author feels that great expertise as a writer is to be gained

A. very quickly, that is in a few days or weeks,
or
B. through sustained work over a few years?

236. If the beginning writer demands from himself or herself high performance on all, or almost all, of these tasks at the same time, the process can be very unpleasant. There isn't enough working memory in the brain to

pay attention to all of these at once. You need to figure out ways to practice them separately, working toward fluency and automaticity in as many as you can. The more of these you are fast and automatic in, the more you can free up your brain's resources to think about what you're trying to say and how to communicate it best. Even then, it's good to do writing in stages, where you concentrate on one task at a time as much as possible.

This section deals with the following problem:

A. that there will always be people who will criticize what you have written,
or
B. that writing involves so many component skills that if developing writers try to pay attention to all at once, there isn't enough memory to go around?

237. As you write, I recommend going in GIOW order: generation, inclusion, ordering, and wording. You first generate a bunch of ideas. Then you decide which to include and which to leave out. Next, you put them in the best order you can. Finally, you make the wording as clear and pleasant to read as you can make it – thinking about grammar, punctuation, and so forth. When you are focusing on one task, you try not to worry about the others. For example, when you are generating ideas, you silence the comments your internal critic might have about inclusion, ordering, or wording.

The main point of this section is that

A. when writing, it's best to focus on one thing at a time rather than to try to do everything at once,
or
B. generating ideas is the stage of writing where you get to be truly creative?

238. Keeping your internal critic under control is a very important way to keep writing from being unpleasant. When you begin to write something, you will often need to tell your "internal critic" to relax and leave you alone for a

while. For example, someone starts writing, and before the first sentence is even done, a little voice in the head starts saying, "This is an awkward sentence. How could you begin your composition this way? You've probably got some grammar errors already. Are you sure you spell this word that way? If people read this, you'd really be embarrassed."

The purpose of this section is to

A. explain and illustrate what is meant by the "internal critic,"
or
B. explain why people develop an "internal critic" in the first place?

239. Using the internal critic too strongly causes people to get blocked from writing – often writing just comes to a standstill. You need to silence the internal critic at least until you get lots of words written down. After you have a draft to work from, you can start looking for flaws and correcting them. But even then, you want to celebrate and feel good about every improvement

that you make, and not get down on yourself for the imperfections that you find. You want to say things to yourself that make the process of writing as pleasant as possible.

The major point of this section is that

A. especially when you're beginning a certain piece of writing, turn down the internal critic so that writing doesn't get to be unpleasant,
or
B. turning down the internal critic doesn't mean you should be content with bad writing?

240. Here's another tip for becoming a better writer. Every time you read something, you are getting a model of how someone wrote. Pick out writing that you like, and that other people think is good, and try to notice why it works. How did the writer do it? Did the writer come up with really good ideas? Did the writer put the ideas into an order that made things clear? How did the writer organize the ideas? What

vocabulary and what sorts of sentences did the writer use? You can even take time to reread portions and notice how the writer punctuated the sentences. Rather than just thinking about the content of the writing, you are looking for any tricks of the writing trade that you can pick up from one of the masters.

A summary of this section is

A. it's good to examine good writing with the goal of learning how to write well,
or
B. we learn a good fraction of everything we know by observing models of what other people have done?

241. When you do this, you don't need to confine yourself to writing that is considered "great literature." Most of the writing that most people do in their lives is nonfiction. Notice the writing in your textbooks. Often textbooks provide excellent models of how to explain things clearly and concisely.

In this section, the author is advising including as models books with titles like

A. *General Science*, *World History*, and *Introduction to Psychology*,
or
B. *Hamlet*, *Romeo and Juliet*, *Moby Dick*, and *17th Century British Poetry*?

242. Here's a writing exercise that will accomplish several things at once. This is what I've referred to as the reflections exercise, in writing. You pick up one of your textbooks, one of your literature books, or any other book you consider important, and you carefully read a paragraph. Then you put the book aside, and without looking at it, you write what you remember from it. You don't have to worry about plagiarism in this exercise – if you liked the author's wording and you can remember it, you are free to write it down. Usually you will have no choice but to put what you remember into your own words. You will get plenty of practice in figuring out how to put

the ideas into words. If you want to imitate the writer's style, that's great. But you are not writing notes – you're writing complete sentences, in a well-organized paragraph.

Following the advice in this section allows you to

A. focus on remembering and wording some ideas without having to think up new ideas,
or
B. focus on generating new ideas without worrying about wording?

243. After you've written, you look back at the paragraph in your book, and you compare the author's version with your version. If the author's version is more masterful than yours, don't get down on yourself, but celebrate that you've noticed differences that will help you the next time.

Then you repeat this process with the next paragraph. As you do this, you're mastering whatever you're reading, as well as becoming a better writer.

The sequence advised in the previous two sections is to

A. preview the whole section of text, then read it, then make up questions about it, then review it again,
or
B. read a paragraph, summarize it in writing, compare your writing to the original, and move to the next paragraph?

244. How do you learn to put together good sentences? I think that exercises in sentence combining are very useful for this component skill for writing. There are several books of these exercises available. Here's how an exercise goes. You have a set of sentences like this:

He wanted a software program. It was called Microsoft Office. But he couldn't afford it. So he downloaded OpenOffice.org. It was free. It suited him just as well.

Your job is to combine these choppy sentences into one sentence, such as this:

Unable to afford the Microsoft Office software he wanted, he found that a free download of OpenOffice.org suited him just as well.

The main point of this section is that when you do the sentence combining exercise,

A. the input is a set of simple sentences and the output is a more complex sentence,
or
B. you can think up your own simple sentences in addition to using those that others have made up as exercises?

245. When you deliberate how to combine simple sentences into longer ones, you do something very central to the writer's craft. Almost every sentence that you write will involve combining ideas in ways that feel very much like a sentence combining exercise.

In this section the author is simply making a pitch that

A. sentence combining exercises help teach you to think like a writer,
or
B. it's good to be constantly on the lookout for ideas to write about?

246. If you like the "programmed" approach to learning in this book, where you read something and quickly answer a question on it, then you should try one of three books by Joseph Blumenthal on English grammar, entitled English 2200, English 2600, and English 3200. Together, these books take you through 8000 tiny exercises meant to make your writing correct and clear. Each one takes a few seconds, and you get much practice as well as great explanations.

This section is really

A. an advertisement for Joseph Blumenthal's grammar books,
or
B. an explanation of how the complex grammar rules of the English language came to be?

247. Like grammar, spelling, typing, and sentence combining, vocabulary deserves separate intensive study over a long time. You pick up vocabulary by reading, but I recommend also systematically studying lists of words and memorizing their meanings. There are many good books that give vocabulary exercises for fairly advanced vocabulary; the *Wordly Wise* series is a good one for the grade school years. You find a vocabulary study series and pick the point in it that is not too hard, not too easy, but just right for where you are now.

The author feels that

A. you should learn words by coming across them in reading and not by studying lists of words, or
B. it's important to gradually add to your vocabulary by studying the meanings of lists of words, appropriate for your level?

248. The hardest part of writing is figuring out something really good to say: something that is so useful, motivating, persuasive, entertaining, or enriching that people don't mind spending their time reading it. Here's my tip for this skill. Open up a word processing file entitled "Ideas for writing." Any time an idea strikes you, jot it down into your idea file. Keep adding to your list of possible things to write that will be useful or creative or fun. Enjoy the fantasy of writing something that lots of people will read. If this fantasy involves becoming, rich, famous, and/or very popular, enjoy it! Enjoy having this fantasy with all sorts of ideas. As you accumulate more ideas, let them compete with one another for the scarce time that you have to actually follow up and write about one of them.

In this section the author advises

A. constantly being on the lookout for ideas to write about, and keeping track of these ideas, or
B. having meditation sessions where you watch what comes into your mind, and notice any ideas worth writing about?

249. If you can have pleasant fantasies of being a successful writer, your fantasies have a pretty good chance of at least partially coming true. Although few people become famous from their writing, millions of people make their living in jobs where writing is a major activity. Walk into a bookstore or library and you might get an impression of how many more authors there are than sports stars. But beyond authors: most other professionals, such as lawyers, scientists, doctors, professors, public relations experts, and others could simply not do their jobs if they didn't have good writing skills.

The main point of this section is that

A. there are millions of jobs where a major activity is writing, or
B. putting all your time into sports leads to a higher chance of getting injured?

250. If you cultivate the mind-set of being constantly on the lookout for good ideas to write about, and trying to remember them, there will be another important effect on your life: you will become a more original thinker. You will gradually cultivate the "life of the mind." You will begin to take more pleasure when a good idea pops into your head. You will see time alone as not a need to get to a TV or videogame as fast as possible, but as a chance to sort through ideas in your head and a chance for some big "light bulbs" to light up inside you. You will more thoroughly enjoy reading, because you will be looking for the ideas that will trigger your own ideas. Being on an idea-search and taking pleasure from each new find is one of the great side benefits of being a writer, whether you are a professional or amateur.

The point of this section is that

A. writing can be a way of making a living, or
B. looking for ideas to write about can open your mind to

experiences that enrich you as a
person?

The Shaping Strategy

251. The word "shaping" means helping someone learn to do a behavior by rewarding the steps of progress toward the goal. Shaping does not involve punishment. You figure out a series of small milestones on the way toward the goal, and you reinforce and celebrate each one of those steps.

The purpose of this section was to

A. define the word *shaping*,
or
B. explain what shaping has to do with being a successful student?

252. Let's imagine that you want teach someone to read. One of the first steps is to have the person practice recognizing words when someone says the sounds separately. So an activity might be to hear sounds like buh-aah-tuh and to hear that the word is *bat*. Another step might be to look at letters and practice saying what sounds the letters make. You cheer and congratulate every bit of practice and progress as the person works on these foundation skills, even though the person is not reading yet. If the person finds any activity frustrating, you find a way to make it a little easier. You don't punish the person. Eventually you go up to having the person sound out easy words, then harder words, and so on. You are using shaping to teach the person to read.

The purpose of this section was to

A. help you teach someone to read,
or
B. give an example of how shaping is used?

253. You can use shaping with yourself. The reward or reinforcement comes from what you say to yourself. Imagine that you have a homework assignment. When you decide to do it now rather than later, you think, "I'm glad I made that decision!" When you get your materials out and sit down with them, you think, "Yay,

I'm getting started just as I planned to!" When you reread what the assignment is, you think "I'm glad I took the time to get straight what I'm supposed to do!" You keep on in this way, all the way to the point where you think to yourself, "I've really mastered this! Plus, I've put my work where I won't forget it! Hooray, I feel good about what I've done!" You've given yourself lots of reinforcement, and you haven't punished yourself. If you can enjoy your own reinforcement, you can have a good time while doing your work!

The main point of this section were that

A. you can use shaping with yourself, while doing academic work,
or
B. even deciding to start working is something worth celebrating?

254. Someone might say, "Why do you make such a big deal over people's enjoying their academic work? The important thing is for them just to do it, even if they

hate it." The answer is simply that our brains are built so that we almost always do things more often if we enjoy them than if we don't. There's something very hard to resist that makes us want to do things that are pleasant and avoid those things that are painful. People can make themselves do painful things for a short time, but if you want to be able to put in the quantity of study necessary to be a successful student, it's important to learn not just to do the work, but to enjoy it.

The main point of this section is that

A. if you're going to be spending lots of time studying, it's important to learn to enjoy that time,
or
B. it's important to be able to do things that you hate doing, if those things are good and useful?

255. Here's a crucial point that many students don't realize: your ability to enjoy a certain type of schoolwork increases the more skilled you are at it. If someone

loves math but dislikes writing, it is probably (but not always) true that the person is much better at math than at writing. So if you dislike a certain subject, you probably need to practice doing it more often. Of course, people tend to practice the subjects they dislike less often, not more often.

Thus the subjects that you are worst in and need to get better in the most are just the ones where the shaping strategy will most come in handy. You say to yourself, "Yay, I used self-discipline in getting started on this subject! ...Hooray, I'm getting more skilled at this!... I'm noticing that it's true, that the faster and more accurately I can do this, the more I enjoy it!"

This section contains the very important point that

A. if you dislike a subject, that probably means you need to practice at it more often,
or
B. it's important to break up your study periods with some exercise, if you are going to enjoy studying most?

256. Mouthing or thinking the words, "Hooray for me, I did a good job on this work," will not be very reinforcing if you do not believe that the work is important or that it will get you something. The more you believe that academic work really is important for the course of your life, the more the thought, "I've just gotten a little better at this academic skill," will make you feel good. Thus if you want your self-shaping strategy to be most successful, look for the pieces of evidence that success in academic subjects makes life better. The evidence is easy to find if you look for it.

The point of this section is that

A. when using self-shaping, it's important to think things like, "Hooray, I've gotten better at an academic skill,"
or
B. sentences like "Hooray, I've gotten better at an academic skill" will only make you feel good if you pay attention to the evidence

that academic skill makes life better?

257. How else can you make your own self-reinforcing sentences more pleasurable for you? How can you get yourself into situations where other people are reinforcing you for academic achievement, and you are enjoying their reinforcement? How can you make it so that you are really having fun working at reading, writing, math, and science?

This book has given many suggestions for the answers to this question. But the person who really has to answer the question is you. If you put your mind to it, and don't give up, you can find it. If you don't ask yourself the question, you won't find it.

"The question" that the author is referring to here is,

A. what's your best use of time, or
B. how can you really enjoy academic work?

258. Many students go through their academic careers groaning and complaining about academic work, doing it only because they feel that someone else is forcing them to. This is no way to live. If there's an activity that will be taking up a huge portion of your first couple of decades of life, you want, if at all possible, not only to do well at it, but also to enjoy doing well at it. Put your intellect and your attention into figuring out how to make it pleasant for yourself, and don't stop until you've succeeded.

A summary of this section is that

A. the most important thing about academic work is that it will help you make the world a better place, or
B. keep trying until you've figured out not only how to do academic work well, but also how to enjoy doing it well?

Index

Index

www.ingramcontent.com/pod-product-compliance
Lightning Source LLC
Chambersburg PA
CBHW081151090426
42736CB00017B/3273